Explore Britain's

Historic Houses

※

D1404186

Produced by AA Publishing

EXPLORE BRITAIN'S
HISTORIC HOUSES

by Penny Hicks

Copy Editor: Rebecca Snelling

Published by AA Publishing, a trading name of Automobile Association Developments Limited, whose registered office is Norfolk House, Priestley Road, Basingstoke, Hampshire RG24 9NY. Registered Number 1878835.

A catalogue record for this book is available from the British Library.

ISBN   h/b 0 7495 1049 8
         p/b 0 7495 1095 1

Colour origination by L.C. Repro and Sons Ltd, Aldermaston.
Printed and bound by Graficromo SA, Spain

The contents of this book are believed correct at the time of printing. Nevertheless, the Publishers cannot accept responsibility for errors or omissions, or for changes in details given.

Acknowledgements: all photographs are held in the Automobile Association's own library with contributions as follows:

AA PHOTO LIBRARY with contributions from; F/Cover R. Elliott, Spine R. Fletcher, 8 M. Birkitt, 10 J. Millar, 11 P. Sharpe, 12 H. Williams, 13 M.Trelawny, 15 P. Baker, 16/7 R. Czaja, 17 E. Meacher, 18, 20 N. Ray, 21 T. Teagan, 22 E. Meacher, 23 A. Baker, 24 S. Day, 25 R. Moss, 26/7, 27 S. Day, 28 R. Hayman, 29 A. Baker, 30, 31 H. Williams, 32 W. Voysey, 33 R. Newton, 34 H.Williams, 35 P. Baker, 36, 37 H.Williams, 38, 39 S. Day, 40, 41 R. Moss, 42 A. Besley, 44 H. Williams, 45 A. Lawson, 46 M. Birkitt, 47 R. Newton, 48 M. Birkitt, 49, 50/1 W. Voysey, 51 A. Lawson, 52/3 V. Greaves, 53 N. Ray, 54 D. Noble, 55 D. Forss, 56 M. Birkitt, 57 R. Mort, 58 D. Forss, 59 S & O Matthews, 60 J. Millar, 61 M. Trelawny, 62 R. Mort, 63 D. Forss, 65 D. Noble, 66 W. Voysey, 67 R. Strange, 68 F. Stephenson, 69 M. Adelman, 70, 71 M. Trelawny, 72 M. Birkitt, 73 F. Stephenson, 74 S & O Matthews, 75 W. Voysey, 76 M. Trelawny, 77 D. Forss, 78, 79 S & O Matthews, 80 D. Forss, 81 F. Stephenson, 82/3 W. Voysey, 84 F. Stephenson, 85 S & O Matthews, 86 W. Voysey, 88 T. Woodcock, 89 J. Wyand, 90 P. Baker, 92, 93, 94 M. Birkitt, 95 R. Surman, 96, 97 S & O Matthews, 98 R. Newton, 99 M. Trelawny, 100 R. Newton, 101 M. Trelawny, 102 M. Birkitt, 103, 104 R. Surman, 105 A. Lawson, 106 D. Forss, 107 H. Williams, 108, 109 J. Welsh, 110, 111 R. Newton, 112 I. Burgum, 113 R. Newton, 114 I. Burgum, 115 R. Newton, 116 R. Eames, 117 R. Newton, 118 M. Allwood-Coppin, 119, 120/1 I. Burgum, 122 V. Greaves, 123 R. Newton, 124 R. Surman, 125 V. Greaves, 126, 127 L. Whitwam, 128 P. Sharpe, 129 E. Bowness, 130, 131, J. Beazley, 132 J. Loan, 133 J. Morrison, 134 J. Mottershaw, 135 E. Bowness, 136 P. Sharpe, 137 L. Whitwam, 138 S & O Matthews, 139, 140 J. Beazley, 141 M. Alexander, 142 R. Weir 142 J. Beazley, 143 D. Corrance, 144 J. Beazley, 145 J. Henderson, 146 R. Weir, 147 J. Carney, 148, 149 J. Beazley, 150 P. Sharpe, 151 S. Day, 152 J. Beazley, 153 D. Corrance, 154 D. Hardley, 155 D. Corrance, 156 S & O Matthews, 157 J. Beazley, 158 R. Elliott, 159 J. Beazley,
HATFIELD HOUSE 14, 64 Hatfield House
SPECTRUM COLOUR LIBRARY B/Cover Little Moreton Hall

CONTENTS

Location map
6
Introduction
8

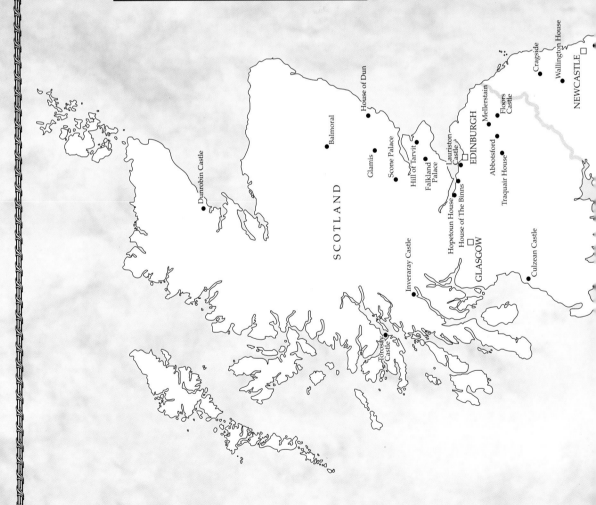

Explore Britain's *Historic Houses*

Location Map

Wallington House

Cragside

NEWCASTLE □

House of Dun

Mellerstain

Floors
Castle

Balmoral

Lauriston
Castle

EDINBURGH

Scone Palace

Glamis

Abbotsford

Hill of Tarvit

Falkland
Palace

Traquair House

Dunrobin Castle

Hopetoun House

House of The Binns

SCOTLAND

GLASGOW

Culzean Castle

Inveraray Castle

Torosay
Castle

Elegant stonework marks the entrance to Knebworth House

$\mathcal{I}$NTRODUCTION

---

*E*ver since the first stately home threw its ornamental gates open to the public, we have been gripped by a fascination for the way the other half – or, more realistically, the other one per cent – lives. But to view only the most splendid mansions is to miss out on one of the most interesting aspects of all, for each and every one of our historic houses – large or small – portrays a social and political history of Britain that no history lesson or learned volume could ever convey.

Many houses provide a journey through time in themselves, beginning as far back as Norman times, perhaps still occupied today by the same family and with every stage of the intervening years apparent in the fabric and contents of the house. Others appear as if halted in time, encapsulating one particular era - a perfectly preserved medieval manor, perhaps, or the great Gothic mansion of a Victorian industrialist – a statement in bricks and mortar of new-found wealth and success.

One frequently overheard comment during tours of historic houses is, '... all this for just one family!' In a way this is true, but it is not something that can be judged by today's standards. These great houses are a relic of a past way of life, and though the descendants of their builders obviously have deep affection for their ancestral homes and feel a duty to maintain them, many present-day owners readily admit to the burdens their heritage has placed upon them.

No-one would consider building on that scale today, but while ostentation certainly played its part in shaping the architectural fashions of the ages, there were practical considerations too.

Not only were families generally much larger, but they would often have a small army of staff to cater for their every need, without the benefits of electrical equipment, easy-care fabrics and convenience food, for example, that we tend to take for granted today. Every lump of coal and pitcher of hot water had to be carried from below stairs to each distant corner of the house, bath water had to be carried back down again and all those acres of carpets had to be cleaned by sprinkling damp tea leaves or pieces of paper over them, then brushing it all up again. (In Victorian times the 4th Marquess of Bath at Longleat even had a man to iron his bootlaces!). The larger of our stately homes could easily have had as many as 50 indoor staff and 30 gardeners.

Entertaining was carried out on a lavish scale, with gargantuan meals emerging from the cavernous kitchens. Nor did friends and family just come for dinner – in the days when horses and carriages were the only means of transport they came to stay, sometimes for weeks on end, bringing their own retinue of personal servants, and all had to be accommodated.

Ornamental candelabras add a touch of opulence to the gallery at Glynde Place

Throughout history these mansions have been at the centre of great estates which were largely self-contained communities, sometimes with their own village for estate workers. What we see today as ornamental parkland would once have been a hunting ground, not simply for sport, but for essential food supplies. There would have been at least one farm, as well as forestry or woodland crafts, a mill, and essential services such as a forge, brew-house, joinery and dairy.

In medieval times, the lord of the manor and his family lived in close proximity to his servants and estate workers. They would all congregate in the huge Great Hall, where all the cooking, eating, entertainment and general living took place. Later came a desire for more privacy and, though life in the Great Hall went on much the same, apartments were added into which the lord and his family could withdraw from the noise and bustle.

In Tudor times great fortunes were made, and the most prominent and powerful families began to gain more of a sense of their own importance. They needed homes to suit their status – and if you were important enough to warrant a royal visit, the monarch would expect proper state apartments, reserved for their use alone, as well as accommodation for their enormous retinue of courtiers and servants. While many members of the aristocracy needed the patronage of

which arose. This was no more so than during the Civil War, when houses designed for peaceful living found themselves besieged and battered. Some escaped war damage only to be sacked by the victorious Parliamentarian forces in retribution for Royalist sympathies.

The geographical location of the house also contributed to the way in which it was built and inhabited. For many centuries no important house was built in the border country between England and Scotland without being properly fortified, as this was an area of disputed territory, with the border moving back and forth with each minor victory, and frequent cross-border raids. Great pele towers were built, which were easy to defend and large enough for the surrounding cottagers to take refuge in times of trouble. Many of the grand houses of Cumbria and Northumberland still have a pele tower at their core. Within Scotland similar struggles over land and property were taking place between the clans, and visits by neighbours frequently heralded not inconsiderable bloodshed. Many of the great mansions along the Welsh border began as castles – outposts of the Norman conquerors, where loyal knights stood at arms against any insurgence from the Welsh princes.

Culzean Castle, in a magnificent setting on the Scotland's west coast, was built as a show-home

the monarch to maintain their position – or simply to keep their heads in some instances – most would dread the disruption and crippling costs of a royal visit.

It was during this time that Henry VIII broke with Rome and declared himself head of the church in order to obtain a divorce. Monastic foundations, such as Forde Abbey and Beaulieu, were dissolved and many of these came into private hands to be converted for family living, adding another dimension to our architectural heritage.

Fortunes could change overnight in those days. A change of king – or a king who changed his mind – could make or break a family, and their homes reflected the circumstances

When times became more peaceful within the country, the aristocracy broadened their horizons, and this had an enormous impact on the style of the country house. Young men were dispatched on Grand Tours of Europe in order to improve their minds and their appreciation of the arts. Many returned with huge collections of antiquities and paintings, often with absolutely no thought as to where they would all be put. Houses were extended or rebuilt, and the fashion was to display these treasures in suitably classical surroundings. Tudor and Jacobean façades were swept away in favour of great columned porticoes and sweeping staircases, warm wood-panelled interiors were transformed with marble pillars, intricately decorated plaster ceilings and classical friezes, and special galleries were created to house statues and marbles. Chiswick House, a supreme example of classical style, was either one the of the most impractical houses ever built (it had no kitchen at all), or, more probably, was built primarily as a magnificent showcase for its owner Lord Burlington's collections.

Eighteenth century Wedgwood colours in the dining room at Saltram House, below, contrast with the dark Jacobean beams of Otley Hall, right

Remembered now as a stern and highly moralistic people, the Victorians nevertheless produced some flamboyant and hugely entertaining architecture. Having no taste for the immediate past, and little interest in conservation and heritage, they harked back to a distant age of chivalry, creating fairy-tale Gothic mansions weighted down with pinnacles and heraldic devices, heavy and intricately carved wood panelling and enormously sturdy furniture. The term 'understated' could never have been coined during the 19th century!

Ancient houses which had developed and changed over the centuries were suddenly catapaulted back to their original style, but with added comfort and convenience. Lacock Abbey is one example of a house where original monastic features can be seen alongside Gothic Revival additions. As well

The broad and highly carved grand staircase at Hatfield House

as re-shaping existing buildings, the Victorians built some vast new homes, as at Penrhyn in North Wales and at Caerhayes in Cornwall, looking for all the world like genuine Norman castles. This was also the time of the British Empire, when not only vast sums of money were amassed by the ruling classes, but fascinating collections of exotic items found their way into their homes, such as trophies of big game hunting expeditions and intricately carved ivory – neither of which would be considered suitable acquisitions these days. New technology was also beginning to be applied to domestic affairs, with such luxuries as gas lighting and hot water systems.

The Edwardian era brought both the heyday of country house society and its demise. Within a short space of time happy and carefree house parties and

great intellectual gatherings gave way to the fraught times of World War I and a permanent change in the order of our society. After the Great Depression of the 30s and another world war, the nation's workers were far less keen to go 'into service', and by this time many of the owners of our historic houses were also struggling to survive the onslaught of death duties and other taxation.

It was around this time that houses began opening to the public as a serious business venture, a move that was frowned upon by the die-hard aristocracy at the time, but one which many who opposed it at first have copied during the intervening 40 years or so. Although opening their doors to the public began simply as a means of raising much-needed revenue, most owners will readily admit that they enjoy sharing their homes and their heritage with appreciative and interested visitors.

Today there are so many historic houses open to the public that an enormous volume would be needed to include them all. This guide includes a selection which, we feel, covers the whole spectrum from spectacular palaces to delightful little manor houses, from elegant country homes to the romantic turreted castles of Scotland. Every age is covered here from medieval to Edwardian, but this is not just a story of bricks and mortar (nor even of stone and oak timbers), for colourful characters and important historical figures also populate the pages of the book. We hope you will enjoy reading about them as well as visiting their fine old houses.

A view of Chatsworth from the water gardens

BOWOOD
Wiltshire

CALNE, 5 MILES (8 KM) EAST OF CHIPPENHAM

*B*owood is one of the West Country's favourite estates – a fine house set in a wonderful 'Capability' Brown landscape which offers a new delight at every turn. It is occupied today by the Earl of Shelburne, son of the 8th Marquess of Lansdowne, and though he is the first of his family to make Bowood his permanent home the house offers a great insight into the lives of his ancestors and their passion for fine art and literature.

Since the time of the 1st Marquess, in the 18th century, the family has been committed to public service, producing a succession of great men who have distinguished themselves in high political office – a Prime Minister, a Chancellor of the Exchequer, a Governor General of Canada and a Viceroy of India. And yet, in addition to their great involvement in affairs of the state, the successive Lords Lansdowne all found the time to be avid collectors of fine paintings and sculpture, and fascinating heirlooms.

The orangery, designed by Robert Adam and once full of orange and lemon trees, now contains part of the Landsowne collection of paintings and a series of busts, while the sculpture gallery houses a variety of exceptional works, including some collected by the 1st Marquess. The two 16th-century Brussels tapestries on the walls are the

The formal, terraced garden is in complete harmony with the architecture of the house

The graceful Orangery serves as a picture gallery

fairly recent acquisitions of the present Earl of Shelburne. Off the orangery is a small room known as the laboratory, and it was here that Joseph Priestley, tutor to the 1st Lord Lansdowne's two sons, discovered oxygen. John Ingenhouse later discovered the process of photosynthesis in plants here, and carried out pioneering work on smallpox vaccine.

The exhibition galleries upstairs include a fascinating collection of items from the 5th Lord Lansdowne's time in India; the Georgian Exhibition Room is set out as it would have been in the time of the 1st Marquess, complete with figures dressed from the Lansdowne costume collection, while the Victorian Room would have been familiar to the 3rd Marquess. Beyond these is the fabulous collection of family jewels.

Bowood is a splendid house, but it is actually only a part of the building which stood here until as recently as 1955. The house which had developed and expanded with the growing prosperity of its owners over a 200-year period had finally become unmanageable, and in order to save the estate as a whole the 'Big House' was demolished. As a memorial to those great men, however, Bowood is undiminished.

Open from Easter to October daily. Tel: 01249 812102.

Robert Adam's original drawings for what is now the sculpture gallery show pens for wild animals, and family records detail the sad demise of an orang-utan at Christmas in 1768. Jeremy Bentham, the philosopher, visiting the house in 1781, spoke of going to stroke the leopard!

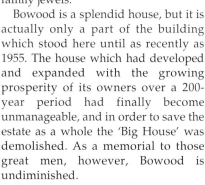

The impressive, romantic castle of Caerhays is set in a famous garden

CAERHAYS CASTLE
Cornwall

GORRAN, 6 MILES (9.5 KM) SOUTH OF ST AUSTELL

Caerhays is a name which was known at the time of the Domesday Book, and though the castle has all the appearance of a great Norman fortress, it is, in fact, a product of the 19th century. It was built for one John Bettesworth Trevanion, who inherited Caerhays in 1801 at the age of 21. It is not clear why Trevanion felt the need for such an impressive new home on land which had been in the family since 1390, nor why he should choose John Nash – very fashionable and very expensive – as his architect. What is known for sure is that the cost of it ruined the family and by 1840 they retreated in debt to Paris, where John died.

The castle then stood empty, rapidly declining, for 13 years until it was bought by Michael Williams, a Cornish Member of Parliament, mine owner and industrialist. He and his son, John, are credited with the restoration of the castle, while the next two generations created and maintained the delightful gardens and grounds which surround it. Now in its fifth generation, the Williams family is still at Caerhays.

Today there are few reminders of the Trevanions, apart from a number of family portraits, and most of the furniture is modern.

Open between March and May on selected days. Tel: 01872 501310.

CLEVEDON COURT
Avon

1½ MILES (2.5 KM) EAST OF CLEVEDON

*T*his is a remarkably complete 14th-century house, and one of the oldest of its type to have survived anywhere in Britain. Incorporated into it is an even older tower which had been built as a defence against marauding Welsh from across the Bristol Channel. Later additions and modifications have only added to the charm of Clevedon Court, without detracting from the fact that it is still considered to be typical of the medieval period.

The focal point of the medieval manor house was the Great Hall, which was divided by a screen passage. On one side was the buttery and kitchen, on the other the main body of the hall, used as the general living area of the household. Beyond that were the living quarters of the lord of the manor and his family. Clevedon Court also retains its early 14th-century chapel, situated on the first floor, which has beautiful and intricate tracery.

In the 18th and 19th centuries Clevedon became a meeting place for the *avant-garde* of the day. One owner during the late Victorian era was Sir Edmund Elton, a celebrated potter, and some of his work is on display in the old kitchen of the house.

Open Easter to September on selected days. Tel: 01275 872257.

The sturdy entrance to Clevedon Court, complete with mock portcullis

COTEHELE
Cornwall

6 MILES (10 KM) SOUTH-WEST OF TAVISTOCK

*I*n the late 18th century Cotehele was already being shown to parties of visitors as a house of antiquarian interest. These visits were instigated by Richard, 2nd Baron Edgcumbe, whose ancestor had built the fortified manor house about 300 years earlier. Although the family had decamped to Mount Edgcumbe by the end of the 17th century, they maintained an abiding interest in their former home and a true appreciation of its historic value. Even the improvements carried out in 1862 for the widow of the 3rd Earl were implemented with a sensitivity which was rare in Victorian times.

Tucked away at the heart of its 1,289-acre estate in the Tamar Valley, the house has retained much of its medieval plan and a great deal of its medieval atmosphere: there is the Great Hall, hung with arms and armour beneath a high, arched timber roof; the rooms of the original solar block, with fine old furniture and tapestries on the walls; the three internal courtyards; and the fine old kitchen.

The tower was added in 1620 and houses three splendid bedrooms, including King Charles's Room where Charles I is said to have spent a night in the vast four-poster bed. Try to visit the house on a bright day – Cotehele still has no electricity.

Open April to October daily; garden open all year. Tel: 01579 50434/51222.

The tower is a splendid seventeenth-century addition to the old house

The comfortable old library

DUNSTER CASTLE
Somerset

DUNSTER, 2 MILES (3 KM) SOUTH-EAST OF MINEHEAD

Set very picturesquely between Exmoor and the sea, Dunster Castle has every outward appearance of an ancient stronghold with its great towers, turrets and battlements – but in fact these castellations were added in the late 19th century. The castle was built in 1617 and its original fortifications were destroyed after the Civil War, by order of Oliver Cromwell. Thereafter it continued as a fine mansion and many of its handsome features, including intricately decorated ceilings and a superb 17th-century oak staircase, date from the 1680s when a great deal of restoration work was carried out by Colonel Francis Luttrell.

When it was given to the National Trust in 1976, the property had been in the Luttrell family since Elizabeth, Lady Luttrell, bought the Norman castle over 600 years ago. Nothing but the 13th-century gatehouse remains of this original building, but the Luttrell history can be traced on a tour of the castle through fine family portraits, a framed genealogy (not entirely accurate) and a display case of items which belonged to the family.

The dining room and stairhall are particularly grand, and although the morning room may lack their style, it does have wonderful views. The gallery is especially interesting for its leather wall hangings depicting the story of Antony and Cleopatra.

Open from Easter to October daily, except Thursday and Friday. Tel: 01643 821314.

Dunster Castle enjoys an unusually favourable climate and many sub-tropical plants thrive in its beautiful garden terraces, notably a huge lemon tree which bears fruit annually.

The pleasing frontage of Dyrham Park, now in the care of the National Trust

DYRHAM PARK
Avon

DYRHAM, 8 MILES (13 KM) NORTH OF BATH

There was once a Tudor house on this site, but the Dyrham Park we see today, built for William Blathwayt, is entirely a creation of the William and Mary period. Blathwayt rose from fairly modest beginnings through the Civil Service to hold a number of top government jobs and found favour with William III both for his administrative abilities and because he spoke Dutch. Blathwayt also made an advantageous marriage to the heiress of the Dyrham estate, but it was not until after the death of both his in-laws and his wife that he began to replace their family home.

The mansion was constructed in two stages, first in 1692 by an unknown Huguenot architect, and around the turn of the century by one of the foremost architects of the day, William Talman. Between them they created a splendid house which displays unusual restraint for the times.

Dyrham Park has changed little over the years and all the furniture, paintings and pottery we see in the house today were collected by Blathwayt himself. The series of apartments are decorated and furnished very much with a Dutch influence, including paintings of the Dutch school and a collection of blue-and-white Delft ware. There are Dutch-style gardens, too.

Open from Easter to October daily, except Thursday and Friday. Tel: 01272 372501.

FORDE ABBEY
Somerset

4 MILES (6.5 KM) SOUTH-EAST OF CHARD

*T*he radical philosopher Jeremy Bentham, a tenant at Forde Abbey during the 19th century, wrote in a letter, 'Nobody that could stay here would go from hence'. The Cistercian monks who were here until the 16th century would doubtless have felt the same, but Henry VIII's dissolution of the monasteries in 1539 robbed them of any choice in the matter.

After standing empty for 100 years, Forde Abbey became a family home and remains so today. It is unmistakably medieval, despite the efforts of the 17th-century owner who set out to transform the buildings in the style of an Italian *palazzo*. In fact, the monastic layout of its sturdy stone walls was remarkably well suited to that style, and few structural changes were made.

The interiors, however, were panelled and decoratively plastered on a lavish scale: they include the lofty Great Hall, with its oak-panelled ceiling; the ornate grand staircase; and the saloon, with its comfortable seating, elegant drapes and wonderfully preserved Mortlake tapestries. Little has altered here since about 1700 and Forde Abbey is a happy blend of magnificence and utter charm.

Open from April to October on selected days. Tel: 01460 20231.

Five centuries ago monastic chants would have been a not uncommon sound at Forde Abbey. Now famous musicians come from all over the world to record their music in the Great Hall, and the grass slope below Chard's Tower makes a good vantage point to sit and listen.

The mellow stonework of the former abbey blends into its tranquil garden setting

This 20th-century building is a faithful replica of Jacobean style

HAMPTWORTH LODGE
Wiltshire

LANDFORD, 9 MILES (14.5 KM) SOUTH-EAST OF SALISBURY

*H*amptworth Lodge could be said to be a monument to the Arts and Crafts movement of the Edwardian era, despite having the appearance of a Jacobean house. It was actually built in 1912, possibly to the design of the original 1620s house.

Harold Moffatt, who commissioned the new house, was a keen follower of the movement and only traditional building methods were used in its construction, under the direction of architect Guy Dawber – often called 'the Lutyens of the west'. The brick-work designs are particularly notable, and a feature has been made of the rainwater furniture and the diamond-cut inscriptions on some of the leaded windows. The Great Hall is of baronial proportions and has an organ gallery, complete with a huge Willis organ.

The multi-talented Moffatt even went so far as to make much of the furniture himself, and these pieces are also an accurate representation of Jacobean style. There is genuine 17th-century furniture here too, as well as a fine collection of old clocks. The wall coverings are particularly interesting; a variety of woods were used for the panelling, and one room is lined with leather.

Harold Moffatt was a man who was energetically true to his ideals and remains an inspiration to the present owner of the house.

Open all year daily, except Sunday. Tel: 01794 390215.

HEMERDON HOUSE
Devon

2 MILES (3.5 KM) NORTH-EAST OF PLYMPTON

Curiously, the man who built Hemerdon House had a father and father-in-law who shared the same name (Thomas Woollcombe) and the same occupation (surgeons) in the same town (Plymouth). The two were, in fact, related and young George and his wife Maria were cousins. It was Maria who brought the estate into the marriage and the house they built there was begun in 1793.

Delightfully unpretentious, the Georgian house is particularly interesting for the documentation of its occupation kept by successive generations of Woollcombes. Other mementoes of members of the family include the naval uniform and sword of George, son of the original owners, who rose to the rank of Vice Admiral and was wounded at the Battle of New Orleans. His brother, William, fought at Waterloo.

The present owner of Hemerdon, James Woollcombe, has undertaken much restoration in recent years, including the repairing and rebinding of the excellent collection of books in the library, which date from 1546 to the present. Works of art around the house include two portraits by Reynolds, others by Opie and Gand, and some local landscapes.

Open for 30 days between May and September. Tel: 01752 841410.

A pleasing jumble of family photographs and other treasures adorns the piano

ILSINGTON HOUSE
Dorset

PUDDLETOWN, 4½ MILES (7 KM) NORTH-EAST OF DORCHESTER

Below right, the rather severe grey-harled exterior of Ilsington belies its bright interior; above, the elegant dining room

*I*ts royal scandal aside, Ilsington House is more fascinating than its grey, symmetrical façade might suggest, and this is largely due to the splendid restoration work of recent years and the interesting art collection which now adorns its walls. The house is almost pure William and Mary, apart from some 18th-century plaster-work and fireplaces and Victorian additions, and is furnished with fine period pieces.

It was its architectural purity which attracted Peter and Penelope Duff to the house, which they bought in 1979 after an eight-year search for their ideal property. When they moved in a year later, however, they were still without carpets, curtains and furniture as the house had been empty for two years and was in need of restoration, which is an ongoing process. Once in residence, Penelope Duff set about displaying the splendid paintings and sculptures which she had been amassing since the age of 12. It is a fascinating and extensive collection containing both classic and modern works, including signed lithographs by Toulouse Lautrec and a painting of Lew Hoad by Cecil Beaton. There are also a number of works by Peter Mahone, of the Ruralist group, work by Panayiotis Kalorkoti, the official war artist for the Falklands War, and recent works by students of the Royal Academy School. Sculptures include work by Elisabeth Frink and Serena de la Hey.

The scandal involved Princess Sophia, a daughter of George III. Between 1792 and 1830 Ilsington was leased to General Thomas Garth, the King's Principal Equerry who, like many other courtiers, took houses in the area in order to be near the monarch during his summer sojourns in Weymouth. Sophia and two of her sisters would usually spend the last night of their journeys to Weymouth here. In 1800 Princess Sophia gave birth, in Weymouth, to a son who was promptly adopted by a local couple. General Garth adopted the boy when he was two years old and brought him up at Ilsington. Young Thomas received some financial support from his mother, though his attempt to formalise the arrangement came to nothing and in the process he was tricked out of his possession of documents which proved his noble birth. In pursuing his claim further, the scandal broke in the press and the royal family eventually settled £3,000 a year for life on the boy. Though Tom's paternity was never revealed, suspicion fell naturally on General Garth – despite the fact that he was 30 years older than Sophia and far from attractive.

Open from May to September on selected afternoons. Tel: 01305 848454.

The house remains an intriguing record of two remarkable Victorian architects

KNIGHTSHAYES COURT
Devon

BOLHAM, 2 MILES (3 KM) NORTH OF TIVERTON

Though principally famous for its wonderful gardens, Knightshayes Court is well worth a visit in its own right. Its foundation stone was laid in 1869 but it took so long for work to progress that the architect, William Burges, was sacked in 1874 and J D Crace was appointed to complete the decoration. His painted ceilings and wall stencilling, hidden by later decorations, are being uncovered and restored.

Many of the features installed by Burges also remain, including some delightfully whimsical corbel figures, wood panelling, a great painted bookcase in the stairwell and a series of architectural drawings. In fact, many of the rooms at Knightshayes are an amalgam of the styles of Burges and Crace, endowing them with a unique interest.

The house was built for John Heathcoat-Amory, MP for Tiverton, and remained in the family until the 3rd Baronet, Sir John, died in 1972, leaving the property to the National Trust. The house still contains much of the family furniture and china, together with a collection of Old Masters and some fine family portraits.

Of particular interest is the Golf Room, which illustrates Lady Heathcoat-Amory's golfing career. As Miss Joyce Wethered, she was four-times winner of the Ladies Open in the 1920s.

Open April to October on selected afternoons. Tel: 01884 254665/257381.

LACOCK ABBEY
Wiltshire

LACOCK, 3 MILES (5 KM) SOUTH OF CHIPPENHAM

When Lacock Abbey was given to the National Trust in 1944 it came with a whole village, and a more delightful and complementary assemblage would be hard to find. The abbey was founded in 1232 and continued as an Augustinian nunnery until Henry VIII dissolved the monasteries in 1539.

Like many other religious foundations, Lacock was converted into a private residence, but unlike most others it has retained a large proportion of its monastic buildings, including the cloisters, chapter house and sacristy. And where many similar properties were changed beyond recognition, Lacock was converted with care and sensitivity, though some of its features are Gothic Revival rather than pure medieval. It is furnished with some interesting pieces, including a chair which is said to have been used in the camp of Charles I, and a pair of 18th-century leather chests. Also on display is a photographic copy of the Lacock Abbey Magna Carta (the original is in the British Museum).

For most of its secular life Lacock Abbey was owned by the Talbot family, whose most famous member was William Henry Fox Talbot, the pioneer of photography who invented the photographic negative here. The middle window in the south gallery was the subject of Fox Talbot's earliest existing negative, and there is a Museum of Photography in the gatehouse.

Open from Easter to October every afternoon, except Tuesday. Tel: 01249 730227.

Fine vaulting adorns the old cloisters

LANHYDROCK HOUSE
Cornwall

2½ MILES (4 KM) SOUTH-EAST OF BODMIN

*L*anhydrock House could easily have looked very different indeed to the lovely, symmetrical Tudor mansion ranged around three sides of a courtyard that we see today. The fact is that only the north wing, entrance porch and gatehouse are original. The rest of the 17th-century house was destroyed by fire in 1881, at a time when all too often the conservation of the past was sacrificed to Victorian enthusiasms. Fortunately, the owner, Lord Robartes, had the house rebuilt in the exact style of the remaining portion, using the same grey granite and recreating what is one of the most delightful compositions in the country.

Inside, though, it is pure Victoriana and a tour of the house gives a vivid insight into the lives of both the owners and their staff in those times. The 'below stairs' parts of the house are fascinating, and include an enormous kitchen with its larders and a dairy, still with the equipment and utensils required to feed a great household. The tour also includes the bakehouse, cellars and the servants' quarters. Of the grander apartments, the Long Gallery, in the original wing, is particularly splendid. It is 116ft (35m) long and has an intricately carved plasterwork ceiling depicting scenes from the Old Testament, worked by local craftsmen in the mid-17th century. Throughout, the house is furnished in fine style with some lovely 18th-century furniture and tapestries.

The house was given to the National Trust in 1953, having belonged to the Robartes family since 1620 when Sir

Symmetrical wings give Lanhydrock a particular air of formality

Richard Robartes, a Truro banker, bought the estate. In 1624 James I made him a baron, which may have prompted the building of the house. The beginning of construction work certainly coincided with the bestowing of the title. Unfortunately, Sir Richard did not live to see his beautiful home completed and it was left to his son to finish the work.

The gatehouse, another survivor from the original building, now stands alone as the main entrance to the house and the formal Victorian gardens. These cover some 22 acres (9ha) and consist of herbaceous borders and formal parterres, with clipped yews and bronze urns. There are also beautiful rhododendrons, camellias and magnolias. Beyond the gardens, the estate extends to around 1,000 acres (400ha) of meadows and woodland, with a network of footpaths.

Open from April to October daily, except Monday, but open Bank Holiday Mondays. Tel: 01208 73320.

The intricate ceiling of the famous Long Gallery shows Old Testament scenes

The splendid old Elizabethan house of Longleat has seen many changes, including the development of a safari and wildlife park in the grounds

LONGLEAT
Wiltshire

5 MILES (8 KM) WEST OF WARMINSTER

The man who built Longleat was truly remarkable. In the space of just 40 years John Thynne rose from working in Henry VIII's kitchen to entertaining Queen Elizabeth I at his vast mansion. Single-mindedly ambitious and cleverly persuasive, he acquired both social position and great wealth and laid the foundations of a dynasty which still occupies the vast country estate originally purchased for £53. When the new house, which he designed himself, was destroyed by fire the determined Thynne simply bought a quarry of Bath stone and started again.

Colourful characters have always populated Longleat. John Thynne's son, a lazy and violent man, was fined for fraud and the mismanagement of his public duties; a later heir married a woman who, though of noble birth, was so disreputable that her behaviour shocked even Charles II and she was banned from Court; the next heir was murdered by assassins hired by an admirer of his wife; another eloped with the daughter of a local toll-keeper. And yet, though so many of the guardians of Longleat could easily have led caused its downfall, every so often there came a descendant who was worthy of John Thynne. The 1st Viscount Weymouth was such a man. Of modest habits and a devoted husband, he built up the estate and created wonderful gardens, sadly destroyed in one generation by his successor who neglected both house and grounds. The 3rd Viscount found favour at the Court of George III, who elevated him to the rank of Marquess of Bath and visited Longleat in 1789. Nevertheless he died in debt and his son, a shrewd businessman, was forced to concentrate all his efforts on saving the estate. He also made substantial improvements to the house, employing James Wyatt to carry out the work which took ten years to complete.

In the history of such a family as this it is difficult to pick out a 'Golden Age', but the Victorian era certainly left its mark here. The estate prospered, high society was lavishly entertained and the state rooms were remodelled in baroque style, with no expense spared. The excellent workmanship is still evident today in the superbly intricate gilded ceilings and the extraordinarily sumptuous and richly decorated rooms. But the development of Longleat did not stop there – the present Lord Bath's apartments are decorated with his own murals, hugely colourful works which display a characteristic lack of restraint.

Open all year daily, except Christmas Day. Tel: 01985 844400.

The lower dining room features a remarkable gilded ceiling

THE MANOR HOUSE
Devon

SHUTE BARTON, 3 MILES (5 KM) SOUTH-WEST OF AXMINSTER

Shute Barton Manor has the largest fireplace in England – possibly in the world – which at 22ft (6.6m) by 7ft (2.1m) stretches across the entire end wall of the entrance hall.

The imposing gatehouse

Set back from a narrow country road and dominating the heart of the tiny village, the Tudor gatehouse leading to Shute Barton Manor could hardly be more impressive. The manor itself is both an important historic monument and an utterly charming family home, for although it is in the care of the National Trust, the Carew Pole family still live there and amidst the ancient stone walls and antique furniture there are family photographs, dogs and the paraphernalia left by visiting grandchildren.

Shute Barton is one of Britain's most important surviving non-fortified manor houses, and the earliest building here dates from about 1380. It was extended in the 15th century by the Greys, Marquesses of Dorset, who remained here until, in 1554, the entire family fell from grace when they failed to install Lady Jane Grey upon the throne. The Pole family leased, then bought the manor, later making substantial changes. However, its ancient origins are very much apparent today, particularly in the solar, with its exposed roof timbers and two garderobes. Other rooms have been furnished for family use and contain lovely old pieces of furniture and interesting paintings.

Open from April to October on selected afternoons. Tel: 01297 34692.

MONTACUTE HOUSE
Somerset

MONTACUTE, 4 MILES (6.5 KM) WEST OF YEOVIL

Montacute House, a beautiful home rescued from the scrap heap

Montacute House is one of Britain's best-preserved Elizabethan mansions – an impressive edifice of glittering glass interspersed with the golden glow of Ham Hill stone. It was built around the end of the 16th century for Sir Edward Phelips, a lawyer who rose to be Speaker of the House of Commons and Master of the Rolls (it was he who opened for the Prosecution at the trial of Guy Fawkes).

The interior of the house is no less impressive than its beautiful, symmetrical exterior. There are decorated ceilings, splendidly ornate fireplaces, heraldic glass and fine wood panelling, but by the time the property came to the National Trust the original contents had, sadly, been dispersed. In fact, the house itself was nearly lost – in 1931, after years of neglect, it was on the market for £5,882 'for scrap'! Rescue came in the form of a Mr E Cook who donated sufficient funds to the Society for the Protection of Ancient Buildings to buy Montacute and to present it to the National Trust.

Today, the rooms are suitably furnished thanks to various loans and bequests, and the Long Gallery – at 172ft (52.2m) the largest surviving gallery in the country – houses a magnificent collection of Elizabethan and Jacobean paintings on permanent loan from the National Portrait Gallery.

Open from Easter to October daily, except Tuesday. Tel: 01935 823289.

MOMPESSON HOUSE
Wiltshire

SALISBURY, 21 MILES (34 KM) NORTH-WEST OF SOUTHAMPTON

Hailed as a perfect example of Queen Anne architecture, Mompesson House presents a distinguished façade in this secluded and exclusive neighbourhood – the peaceful, elegant cathedral close. The close is encircled by 14th-century walls which have three sturdy gateways and these are still locked every night.

Mompesson House was built in 1701 for Charles Mompesson, the local Member of Parliament, and was much improved about 40 years later by his brother-in-law (and heir), Charles Longueville, who redecorated the rooms and added the elegant oak staircase and the decorative plasterwork. This is seen at its best around the stairwell, where every surface is covered with intricate scrolls and motifs.

The house is furnished throughout in appropriate style. The dining room, with 18th-century mahogany furniture, has a sparkling array of silver and is set with fine Sèvres and Coalport china. A display cabinet contains lovely Derby and Bow figures, while another huge cabinet houses a display from the collection of 18th-century drinking glasses bequeathed by Mr O Turnbull. There are over 370 items in the collection, and every one is different. The drawing room is the grandest room of all, with not only

The pleasant façade of Mompesson looks out on the Cathedral Close

The magnificently carved staircase leads up from the entrance hall

some of the best plasterwork and an impressive chimneypiece, but also works from the Watney bequest of Dutch flower paintings. There is a beautiful cut-glass chandelier, and in a fine mahogany cabinet is part of the Bessemer Wright collection of English porcelain.

The Green Room ceiling features an enormous eagle with outspread wings looking down on the fine walnut furniture and a collection of mezzotints and 17th-century stumpwork pictures, while the 'little' drawing room contains a display of photographs and souvenirs of Miss Barbara Townsend, whose family lived here for about 100 years. Its walls are usually covered with blue-and-white Chinese and Delft dishes, but this room often houses temporary exhibitions.

The most recently opened room in the house is the library, which reflects the ownership of Denis Martineau, who donated the property to the National Trust. Sadly, most of the contents had already been dispersed, and the furnishings seen today come mainly from other sources, but in the library there is an architectural drawing of the Royal Crescent in Bath by Martineau, and the décor of this room reflect his taste.

Open from Easter to October every afternoon, except Thursday and Friday. Tel: 01722 335659.

The parlour is dominated by the strange painting of hares taking their revenge on huntsmen

NEWHOUSE
Wiltshire

REDLYNCH, 8 MILES (13 KM) SOUTH OF SALISBURY

Newhouse is one of only two 'Trinity' houses in Britain – houses built in the shape of a Y to represent the three arms of the Trinity. Curiously, the other house, in Herefordshire, is also called Newhouse.

I n 1986 George and June Jeffreys inherited a near-derelict Jacobean house which was on the verge of being condemned, but in a relatively short space of time they have restored both house and gardens to make a delightful family home. On the dining room table, displayed among old documents and mementoes of Nelson, visitors can trace the changes which have taken place here through a series of old photographs.

A daughter of one of the Jeffreys' ancestors was related to the great admiral by marriage, and his daughter by Emma Hamilton was brought up at Newhouse – her cot, made by a ship's carpenter, can be seen in one of the bedrooms. The dining room is also the venue for the annual 1805 Dinner held to commemorate Nelson.

The house contains some fine old pieces of furniture and a library of books which date back at least to 1576. There is also a small costume collection, one of the dresses on display being depicted in a painting above it. There are many family portraits around the house but perhaps the most intriguing item is the 'Hare' picture, dating from 1640, which depicts hares triumphing over huntsmen. It is not certain whether the artist was an animal rights sympathiser, or whether there was a religious or political significance in the unusual portrayal.

Open daily in August. Tel: 01725 20055.

PARNHAM HOUSE
Dorset

1 MILE (1.5 KM) SOUTH OF BEAMINSTER

*I*n 1976 this 15th-century manor house was in a state of near-terminal decay and had unsuccessfully been on the market for three years. Then John Makepeace came along. He had been searching for a place in which to establish his School for Craftsmen in Wood and to display some of the finest pieces of contemporary furniture to be made this century. Makepeace has not only set up and expanded his school, but has also splendidly restored Parnham House as a showcase for its work.

If there was ever any doubt as the suitability of an historic manor house as a setting for the most modern of furniture, it is soon dispelled by a tour of the house. The ancient walls, oak panelling and huge windows are a perfect foil for the sleek curves and slender uprights of the finely crafted chairs, tables and cabinets, and imaginative lighting raises the whole ensemble to an art form in itself. In addition to the furniture, there are fine paintings, contemporary ceramics and hand-painted and printed fabrics. John Makepeace's collection of Victorian woodworking tools and wooden artefacts from all over the world are displayed in the library.

Open from April to October on selected days. Tel: 01308 862204.

In the 1920s Parnham was a fashionable country club, and its patrons includied the Prince of Wales and Sir Arthur Conan Doyle. Conan Doyle always stayed in what is now the Country Room, and was convinced that it was haunted.

The mellow old manor house is home to a host of modern treasures

POWDERHAM CASTLE
Devon

POWDERHAM, 6 MILES (9.7 KM) SOUTH OF EXETER

One of the oldest living creatures in the world resides at Powderham Castle. Timothy, the Mediterranean spur-thighed tortoise, is 155 years old and happily inhabits the rose garden at the foot of the east tower. From here he can survey the gardens, parkland and the River Exe.

Powderham Castle, considerably older than it looks, has belonged to the Courtenay family, Earls of Devon, for some 600 years. Most of the alterations and additions to the original house date from the 18th and 19th centuries and it is the elegance of that era which Powderham reflects today.

Originating in France, the Courtenays were related by marriage to the royal house of Valois, and the founder of this line came to Britain with Eleanor of Aquitaine. Later Courtenays have included an Archbishop of Canterbury, a founder Knight of the Garter and even an Heir Presumptive to the throne of England. And yet, if you ask today about famous members of the family, they are just as likely to mention their beloved elderly tortoise as any of these illustrious ancestors! There are many family portraits around the house, including a rather crowded painting of the 2nd Viscount, his wife and their family of 13 daughters and one son. It was the son, the 3rd Viscount, who was instrumental in reviving the Earldom of Devon which had been in abeyance since 1556.

Their Devon home reflects both the passage of time and the changing fortunes of the family from its 14th-century origins through the destruction and rebuilding of the Civil War period to the age of Victorian grandeur. The dining hall, though the most recent addition, is where the family history can be explored through a series of coats of arms going back to about AD1000. The Marble Hall is particularly interesting – it forms the lower half of the medieval Great Hall and still contains the three original arches, though they were plastered at a later date. This room would once have been as high as the staircase hall, with its fine mahogany staircase adorned with carved heraldic beasts and lavish plasterwork; it was completed in 1755 at a cost of £355.14s.0d.

Upstairs, the solar, once the family room of the medieval castle, has a charming collection of toys including a model Tudor house which was made by a retired estate worker. The rest of the house is an enchanting mixture of original medieval features, family portraits, splendid 18th-century decoration and little curiosities such as the narwhal's horn in the first library (listed in old inventories as a unicorn's horn), and the peacock ornament from the Empress of China's sedan chair at the top of the grand staircase.

Open from April to September daily, except Saturday. Tel: 01626 890243.

Left, the elegant, high-ceilinged music room, and below, the painted stairwell

In ancient times St Michael's Mount may well have been the isle of Ictis, which was known to Greek travellers and merchants. It was for many years an important port, not only for the export of Cornish tin, but also for trade in Irish gold and copper.

ST MICHAEL'S MOUNT
Cornwall

MOUNTS BAY, ½ MILE (1 KM) OFFSHORE FROM MARAZION

Like its ciunterpart in France, St Michael's Mount is set on an island close to the shore

An old Cornish legend claims that in the 5th century some fishermen saw the Archangel St Michael on a ledge of rock on the western side of the Mount, and it has been called St Michael's Mount ever since. The legend of Jack the Giant-Killer also originated here: the giant Cormoran was said to have built the Mount, from where he waded ashore to steal cows and sheep from the locals. Jack rowed out to the Mount one night and dug a great pit while the giant slept. The next morning Cormoran awoke and set off towards the shore, but fell into the pit – which is still shown to children who visit the Mount.

Legends aside, this great rock is a picturesque sight. Perched upon its summit is a building which has been a church, a priory, a fortress and a private home. It was built in 1135 by the abbot of its namesake, Mont St Michel in Normandy, to whom it had been granted by the Norman Earl

of Cornwall. However, the original building was destroyed by an earthquake in 1275. It was difficult, with their French connection, for the monks of St Michael's Mount to prosper during the intervening years as England was constantly at war with France.

For all its isolation, the Mount was seen as strategically important whenever there was turmoil in the country – the Wars of the Roses, the Prayer Book Rebellion, the Armada and, of course, the Civil War, when it was a Royalist stronghold until surrendered to Parliament in 1646, and subsequently taken over as a garrison.

When the military left, the Mount came into the private ownership of the St Aubyn family, but in the days when travel was arduous and social connections were paramount it left much to be desired. In fact, the Mount remained largely unoccupied, used only occasionally during the summer, until the late 18th century when the family began to look upon the Mount as a more permanent residence. Undaunted by the fact that the living quarters were not of an adequate size, they set about the construction of a great new wing – not an easy task on a great rock which is cut off at every high tide.

The St Aubyns were obviously a force to be reckoned with and the splendid Victorian apartments that they added are as much a testament to their determination as to their good taste. There are some fine plaster reliefs, beautiful Chippendale furniture and collections of armour and pictures.

Open from April to October on weekdays. Tel: 01736 710507.

Saltram overlooks the lovely Plym estuary

SALTRAM HOUSE
Devon

2 MILES (3 KM) WEST OF PLYMPTON

'The place is a thousand times more delightful than all the possibility of my imagination had conceived, it is so gay, so riant, so comfortable and so everything that it ought to be that it is impossible to love and admire it enough'.
Countess of Morley, wife of the 1st Earl

Joshua Reynolds was a friend of Lord Borington and, in return, Borington was one of his best customers – there are no less than ten portraits by Reynolds at Saltram House, dating mostly from the 1770s.

This substantial mansion is famous for its splendid Adam interiors and for having some of the best-preserved rooms of their kind in the country.

It was Lord Boringdon who employed Robert Adam to embellish the house which his grandfather, George Parker, had bought in the early 18th century. The saloon and the dining room are undoubtedly the best rooms in the house, illustrating both the skill of the architect and his attention to detail. He not only designed rooms, but created a unified whole in minute detail, specifying pieces of furniture and marking where paintings should be hung – even what their subject matter should be. Some of his original drawings may be seen on display.

There are lots of rooms to see at Saltram, including the intimate entrance hall, the delightful morning room and Velvet Drawing Room, the Chinese Chippendale Bedroom and its similarly styled dressing room, the library with its fine collection of leather-bound books, and the Mirror Room with its Chinese mirror paintings and lovely collection of ceramics. The Great Kitchen, dating from 1778, is a fascinating showplace of domestic pride – and drudgery – with a collection of some 600 sparkling copper pans, an enormous open fireplace and a cast-iron closed range which was installed in 1885.

Open from April to October every afternoon, except Friday and Saturday. Tel: 01752 336546.

STANWAY HOUSE
Gloucestershire

STANWAY, 3 MILES (5 KM) NORTH-EAST OF WINCHCOMBE

New stables were built at Stanway in 1859. The original block, to the east of the barn and next to the churchyard, was abandoned because worshippers were disturbed by 'the oaths of the strappers'.

*B*uilt of golden limestone when Queen Elizabeth I was on the throne, Stanway House is not only an outstanding example of Jacobean architecture, it is also a fascinating portrayal of the development of the manor house of a Cotswold squire. Richard Tracy, whose family had owned land in the county since before the Conquest, obtained the lease from the Abbot of Tewkesbury in 1530 – the only time that Stanway has changed hands in the last 1,260 years. It is now the home of Lord and Lady Neidpath whose ancestor, Lord Elcho, married the last Tracy heiress. It is said that he died of an overdose of punch.

There is a sense of continuity at Stanway; it is still very much a lived-in family home and remains the heart of the community. Having resisted the temptation to sell off its cottages, it is one of very few estates to which tenants bring their rent in person on a quarterly basis, handing over the sums due at a 250-year-old table in the Audit Room. The tour of this beautiful house is taken under the watchful eye of generations of family portraits, people who have helped to preserve and perpetuate what is one of the most romantic houses in Britain.

Open from June to September on selected afternoons. Tel: 01386 73469.

The ornate gatehouse at Stanway is beautifully decorated with a shell motif

Few prominent families with such a long history are without in the occasional black sheep. For the Herberts, this was the 7th Earl, who not only sank the family into debt but was twice accused of murder. Eventually found guilty of manslaughter, he was incarcerated in the Tower.

WILTON HOUSE
Wiltshire

WILTON, 3 MILES (4.8 KM) WEST OF SALISBURY

Wilton, the home of a particularly interesting family, is a beautiful house, full of beautiful things. The Herberts, Earls of Pembroke, have been here since the estate was given to William, the 1st Earl, by Henry VIII after his dissolution of the monasteries, and successive generations have cherished their home and built up a wonderful collection of works of art. Their interest in the arts is apparent the moment visitors enter the front hall, for there to greet them is a statue of Shakespeare – the bard received patronage from brothers William and Philip Herbert and dedicated the first folio edition of his plays to them. This involvement in the arts has continued to the present day, for the present (17th) earl is a film director and his father was a trustee of the National Gallery, among other similar offices.

The early Herberts tended to marry the sisters of prominent figures of their time – the 1st Earl married the sister of Catherine Parr, sixth wife of Henry VIII, which played some part in his rapid rise at Court. His son Henry, the 2nd Earl, married the sister of Lady

Below, the Palladian bridge across the Nadder

Jane Grey, but this marriage was annulled when the Grey family fell from grace; his second wife was the sister of Sir Philip Sidney, the great Elizabethan poet.

After a disastrous fire in the 17th century much of the house was rebuilt to designs by Inigo Jones. His masterpiece here is the magnificent Double Cube Room which has a superb painted ceiling, gilded plasterwork and fine furniture – and every painting is by Van Dyck, or from his studio. The Single Cube Room is equally sumptuous but smaller, measuring 30ft (9m) in every direction. The Colonnade Room, formerly the state bedroom, is more delicate and houses family portraits by Reynolds. In complete contrast, the large smoking room is fairly plain, except for its elaborate Chippendale cabinet and the delightful collection of 55 paintings of the Spanish *haute école* riding school. The Gothic hall and upper cloisters are different again – part of the work completed in the early 19th century by James Wyatt.

The old riding school at Wilton has now been converted into the Exhibition Hall, where an entertaining film on the lives of the Earls of Pembroke may be seen. After the grandeur of Wilton's state apartments, the reconstructed Tudor kitchen gives an insight into the realities of life in those days.

Open from April to October, daily. Tel: 01722 743115.

Steeped in older history, Wilton was also the unlikely setting of the Southern Headquarters for the D-Day Landings

Tradition has it that the first performances of *Twelfth Night* and *As You Like It* were performed at Wilton by Shakespeare himself and his own company of players.

AUDLEY END
Essex

1 MILE (1.5 KM) WEST OF SAFFRON WALDEN

'Too large for a king, but might do well for a Lord Treasurer.'
James I

The elaborate Great Hall

When it was first built around two great courts in the early 17th century, Audley End was one of the largest houses in England. The estate was given to Lord Audley by Henry VIII after he had dissolved the abbey which stood on the site, but it was Audley's descendant, Thomas Howard, 1st Earl of Suffolk, who commissioned the enormous Jacobean house.

Still impressive, the house we see today is, in fact, less than half the size of the original, for much was demolished during the 18th century when Vanbrugh was employed to remodel the house. Fortunately, the architect left the exterior of the house as it was, with its balustraded and turreted roof intact, and made no change to the Great Hall which still retains its wonderfully carved screen and panelled ceiling. Most of the house, though, reflects the tastes of a later age.

Audley End became a royal residence when Charles II purchased it for £50,000 in 1669, and it was also used by James II and by William and Mary, but by the early 18th century the purchase price had still not been settled in full and the house came back to the 5th Earl of Suffolk.

Open from April to September every afternoon, except Monday and Tuesday. Tel: 01799 522399.

❉

BEAULIEU
Hampshire

BEAULIEU, 7 MILES (11.5 KM) SOUTH-EAST OF LYNDHURST

❉

Beaulieu is a comfortable mixture of ancient and modern

The name of Beaulieu has become synonymous with the National Motor Museum, but behind all this is the lovely and very historic home of Lord Montagu. The house is part of the former Abbey of Beaulieu, the majority of which now forms a splendidly romantic ruin behind the house.

After Henry VIII dissolved the abbey in 1538, the square great gatehouse was converted into a home for the Wriothsley family. In the 18th century, Beaulieu passed by marriage to the family of the Dukes of Buccleuch, and the 5th Duke gave it as a wedding present to his second son, Lord Henry Scott, grandfather of the present Lord Montagu. He extended the house in Victorian Gothic style.

Today the family live in the Victorian wing, but the parts of the house which are on show are delightfully littered with mementoes of four generations. Ancestors gaze down from the walls of the picture gallery, and the entrance hall has objects reflecting the family's interests over the last 100 years.

When the house was enlarged and remodelled, many of the original features were retained and there are some wonderful vaulted ceilings. The family's coronation robes are displayed in the ante room, along with the velvet suit worn by Lord Montagu at the coronation of George VI and Queen Elizabeth.

Open all year daily, except Christmas Day. Tel: 01590 612345.

When Lord Montagu first opened his home to the public in 1952, five historic cars were positioned in the entrance hall to reflect his father's role as a pioneer motorist. That was the basis of what is now one of the finest motor museums in the world.

BLENHEIM PALACE
Oxfordshire

WOODSTOCK, 8 MILES (13 KM) NORTH-WEST OF OXFORD

'We have nothing to equal this.'
George III

This is one of Britain's grandest palaces, an enormous Italianate edifice which covers seven acres (2.8ha) of ground. Between them, the original architect, Vanbrugh, and landscape artist 'Capability' Brown have created breathtaking sights at every turn, from the first glimpse of the palace through the entrance arch to the splendid vista across the lake and its classical Grand Bridge.

The estate and the cost of building the palace was the gift of a grateful Queen Anne to the heroic Duke of Marlborough in thanks for his victory at the Battle of Blenheim. The Duke and his Duchess, Sarah, had long been close friends of the Queen and at the time there seemed no bounds to the monarch's generosity. However, the

Below and right, Blenheim is one of the great palaces of Britain

Duchess later quarrelled with the Queen, lost her place at Court, and royal contributions to the cost of building Blenheim ceased. The Marlboroughs retreated abroad, returning only after the death of Queen Anne to finish Blenheim at their own expense. The path was still not a smooth one, though, for the Duchess also quarrelled with the architect! None of this detracted from the end result, and successive Dukes of Marlborough have maintained and contributed to its grandeur and its wonderful art collection.

Within the house is a stunning series of rooms of magnificent proportions, with rich decoration and many splendid painted ceilings by Louis Laguerre and Sir James Thornhill. There are works of art by Reynolds,

Van Dyck and Kneller, wonderful wood carving by Grinling Gibbons and fine tapestries. The most famous tapestry, in the Green Writing Room, depicts the 1st Duke of Marlborough accepting the surrender at Blenheim. The saloon, which is, in fact, the state dining room, is sumptuously decorated, with ceiling and wall paintings by Laguerre and marble doorframes surmounted by crests. The table is laid with a Minton dinner service, and there is a silver centrepiece of Marlborough on horseback. Connecting with the saloon are three more state rooms, all hung with tapestries of Marlborough's campaigns.

In contrast, many visitors to Blenheim are delighted by the modest little room in which Sir Winston Churchill was born in 1874 (Churchill is the family name of the Dukes of Marlborough, and Sir Winston was cousin to the 9th Duke). Within the 2,100 acres (850ha) of grounds are beautiful formal gardens which have been likened to those at Versailles, an arboretum and a walled garden containing a maze, kitchen gardens and an adventure playground.

Open from mid-March to October daily. Tel: 01993 811091 or 811325 (information line).

In 1988 Blenheim Palace became the fourth site in the United Kingdom to warrant inclusion in the World Heritage List.

Above, swans are the perfect ornament on the moat of this lovely medieval manor house, and right, boxed hedges make an unusual design in the old walled garden

BROUGHTON CASTLE
Oxfordshire

BROUGHTON, 3 MILES (5 KM) SOUTH-WEST OF BANBURY

*O*n a fine summer day, with its golden stone walls reflected in the waters of its moat, it would be hard to find a more picturesque sight than Broughton Castle. It is, in reality, not a castle at all but a splendid medieval manor and most of the original house remains today. There was already a house on the site when Sir John de Broughton built his manor in 1300; then, in the 16th century, it was extended and altered, transforming Broughton into a fine Tudor home. Today, the Great Hall is a curious mixture of medieval stone walls, 16th-century windows and an 18th-century plastered ceiling, and with its suits of armour and an unusual collection of leather buckets it has enormous charm and character.

The oldest part of the house is represented in the groined passage and in the dining room, which was an undercroft in the Middle Ages. There are old stone passageways with vaulted ceilings and grotesque corbel heads at the base of the arches, and a spiral staircase. Another staircase leads to the rare 14th-century chapel with a traceried window, heraldic glass and a fixed stone altar.

The character of the house changes completely in the charming Queen Anne's Room, named to commemorate

a visit by Queen Anne of Denmark, wife of James I, in 1604. It is a light and sunny room with a pretty 18th-century four-poster bed and a splendid fireplace. The King's Chamber, used by both James I and Edward VII, has a remarkable stucco overmantel dating from 1554, and Chinese hand-painted wallpaper. The Oak Room is pure Tudor, with floor-to-ceiling oak panelling and an unusual interior porch, and the gallery has a series of family portraits. The family in question are the Fiennes, Lords Saye and Sele – the present Lord is the 21st Baron – and their lineage can be traced on the family tree in the Great Hall.

William Fiennes was a prominent Parliamentarian during the Civil War, refusing to take the Oath of Allegiance and hosting meetings at Broughton to plan Parliament's opposition to Charles I. He disapproved of the execution of the King, however, and removed himself from public life, an act which earned him a pardon on the Restoration in 1660. Another notable member of the family was Celia Fiennes, remembered for her journals documenting her extensive travels around England at the end of the 17th century.

Open over Easter, then from mid-May to mid-September on selected days. Tel: 01295 262624.

CHARTWELL
Kent

2 MILES (3 KM) SOUTH OF WESTERHAM

'...I never had a dull or idle moment from morning to midnight, and with my happy family around me dwelt at peace within my habitation.'
Winston Churchill

Ceanothus flowers in the gardens of Chartwell

In 1924 Winston Churchill and his family moved to Chartwell and it was to remain their happy home for the next 40 years. It is a modest, Victorian house, but it has become one of the most popular of the National Trust's properties – closer, perhaps, to visitors' own aspirations than any great palace, and certainly of immense interest as the home of one of our greatest statesmen.

At Chartwell, Churchill turned his hand to many things, not only the painting and writing for which he is well known, but also the creation, with his own hands, of the garden walls, rockeries and waterworks, and even the large swimming pool. Today the rooms of the house remain very much as they were in Churchill's day, including his studio containing many of his paintings, and his study, in which he did most of his writing.

The Museum and Uniform Rooms contain a selection of his uniforms and many awards and gifts, as well as a 'wanted, dead or alive' poster issued after his escape from a Boer prison in 1899. Elsewhere around the house are reminders of the great man and his interests – old cigar boxes, a painting of his most successful racehorse, the visitors' book recording the great and famous who came to Chartwell between 1924 and 1964, and portraits of family and friends.

Open from April to November on selected afternoons. Tel: 01732 866368.

The Manor is offset by its magnificent garden

CHENIES MANOR
Buckinghamshire

4 MILES (6.5 KM) EAST OF AMERSHAM

A secret chamber, tunnels leading out into the woods, stories of royal visits – and even a royal ghost – all add to the fascination of this lovely 15th-century manor house. Queen Elizabeth I certainly did sleep here, on a number of occasions, and her father, Henry VIII, brought two of his wives here. They say that his ghostly footsteps can still sometimes be heard, painfully dragging his ulcerated legs along in an attempt to catch his queen, Catherine Howard, in the act of adultery with one of his attendants.

Chenies, built of mellow red brick with stepped gables and some of England's best examples of Tudor chimneys, was the work of the same team of men who enlarged Hampton Court for Henry VIII. The rooms within vary considerably: the oak-floored Queen Elizabeth's Room, with its 16th-century tapestries and furniture; the armoury, a primitive Long Gallery where troops were billeted during the Civil War; the delightful Blue Bedroom with its Chippendale four-poster and other 18th-century furniture; the dining room, modernised in the early 19th century and furnished in contemporary style. The stone parlour, now with 17th-century furniture, is thought to have been the original hall of the 15th-century house.

Open from April to October on selected afternoons. Tel: 01494 762888.

The previous building at Chenies once belonged to Edward I, who used it as a hunting box. Records of one visit in 1296 claim that he brought a camel with him! They also relate that 130 eggs were boiled and distributed to the villagers on Easter Day – possibly the first record of Easter eggs in Britain.

CHICHELEY HALL
Buckinghamshire

CHICHELEY, 2½ MILES (4 KM) NORTH-EAST OF NEWPORT PAGNELL

It would be hard to find bricks put to better use than in the construction of Chicheley Hall – nearly a million were used in the house, its wings and its garden walls – and the pale colour of the pillars, doors and windows contrast to splendid effect. There is yet more contrast inside, as the warmth of the brickwork gives way to the cool, classical entrance hall, then the rich oak panelling of the drawing room, the library and Lord Beatty's study. The Jacobean Room, different again, contains 16th-century fragments from the previous house at Chicheley.

Built for the Chester family between 1719–23, the house had a chequered history, including use by the military and as a school. In 1952 it was bought by the 2nd Earl Beatty who turned it back into a beautiful home. His father, the 1st Earl, was one of the most outstanding and courageous naval commanders of this century. Awarded the DSO at the age of 25, he rose rapidly to become Admiral at the age of 45, and later First Sea Lord. He is, perhaps, best remembered as commander at the decisive Battle of Jutland in 1916. Lord Beatty's study contains his collections, including naval paintings, photographs and copies of his many decorations (the originals are in the Greenwich Naval Museum, London).

Open during April, May and August on Sunday and Bank Holiday afternoons. Tel: 01234 391252.

The warm brickwork of Chicheley Hall, one of the finest 18th-century houses in England

❖

CHISWICK HOUSE
London

BURLINGTON LANE, CHISWICK

❖

A delightfully impractical mansion in the classical style

L ord Burlington, who built Chiswick House in the 1720s, had a passion for the architecture of Ancient Rome, and his creation here is considered to be the finest classical building in the country. Regarded as fanciful and impractical by some of his contemporaries, Burlington's mansion is nevertheless an impressive manifestation both of his skill as an architect and his idealism.

The house is a square, two-storey structure with octagonal rooms at the centre – one above the other, surmounted by a shallow dome – and has two entrances. The modest ground floor entrance is completely overshadowed by the splendid, porticoed first-floor entrance, reached by grand flights of balustraded steps on either side. It is evident from this that the upper floor contained the principal rooms in which to receive guests and entertain friends. And it is thought that the house was always intended for entertainment – there are a number of bedrooms – but there was never a kitchen and meals were either taken in, or brought from the old house near by.

The interior of the house continues the classical style with themes taken from ancient Rome, and has intricately decorated painted ceilings, statues, columns and pedimented door frames.

Outside, the lovely Italianate gardens, with temples and statues, are being restored.

Open all year daily, but closed on Monday and Tuesday between October and March. Tel: 0181-995 0508.

CLANDON PARK
Surrey

WEST CLANDON, 3 MILES (5 KM) EAST OF GUILDFORD

*P*erhaps it is unusual for the tour of a house to begin with its climax, but this is certainly the case at Clandon Park. Its magnificent two-storeyed Marble Hall has a superb plaster ceiling from which the legs of the figures hang down over the classical entablature. The house was built by the Venetian architect, Giacomo Leoni, in about 1733 for the 2nd Lord Onslow, and the series of rooms on show are beautifully proportioned and splendidly furnished.

When the National Trust acquired Clandon Park it was empty and the contents we see today are the result of a generous bequest by Mrs David Gubbay, of Little Trent Park in Hertfordshire. Mrs Gubbay's legacy included the wonderful collection of porcelain which is on display all around the house, the highlights of which include the extraordinarily delicate Commedia dell' Arte figures and a unique and colourful assortment of 17th- and 18th-century Chinese birds. The furniture includes some outstanding examples of marquetry work and there is some fine needle-work on display.

The old kitchen, with its fascinating array of old pots, pans and utensils, and the Museum of the Queen's Royal Surrey Regiment are in the cellar.

In the gardens, which extend to about seven acres (2.8ha), is the delightful Maori House, brought from New Zealand in 1892.

Open from April to October, most afternoons. Tel: 01483 222482.

Clandon's rather austere exterior hides a wonderful marble hall and other treasures

The spectacular Chinese Room

CLAYDON HOUSE
Buckinghamshire

MIDDLE CLAYDON, 5 MILES (8 KM) SOUTH-EAST OF BUCKINGHAM

*I*f 'over the top' had been an expression in use in the 18th century it would almost certainly have been applied to the work of the carver and carpenter Luke Lightfoot, who embellished Claydon House with some of the most fantastic decorative work to be seen in any British house.

His exceptional skill is undisputed, and delicately carved birds and beasts, fruits and flowers spill out of ceilings, cornices, walls and overmantels. The Chinese Room is the most astonishing of all, particularly when it is compared to the restrained, classical-style plasterwork carried out by Joseph Rose in the saloon and staircase hall. The exterior of the house is rather sober, giving no hint of the extravagances to be found within.

The embellishments to the family home were carried out by the 2nd Earl of Verney, apparently in an attempt to score points against his political rival Earl Temple of Stowe. However, his scheme eventually bankrupted him and by 1783 he was forced to sell the house, two-thirds of which was demolished by his successor. Florence Nightingale was a regular visitor to Claydon House – Parthenope Verney was her sister – and the house has a display of relics relating to her Crimean experiences.

Open from April to October, most afternoons. Tel: 01296 730349.

In an attractive downland setting, Glynde is attractively constructed of local materials

GLYNDE PLACE
East Sussex

GLYNDE, 3 MILES (5 KM) SOUTH-EAST OF LEWES

Not to be confused with Glyndebourne, which is just a short distance away, the manor at Glynde has been handed down through generations of the same family for a remarkable 800 years, and they are still here, caring for their lovely home and sharing it with visitors. The medieval house has gone now and the one we see today dates from Elizabethan times, when the property passed by marriage from the Waleys to the Morleys. They built their home not only of the local materials – Sussex flint and blocks of chalk – but also from Caen stone, which was brought in specially from Normandy by boat.

The house later passed, by marriage again, to the Trevor family and one of their descendants was Richard Trevor, Bishop of St Albans and Durham. It was he who remodelled the interior of the house in a more classical style and his Georgian hall, with marbled wooden columns, is particularly notable.

The gallery is at the heart of the house and it is here that the family portraits hang, including a splendid one of the Bishop. All around the house are fine pieces of furniture and paintings, along with items collected by the family over the centuries.

Open May to September on selected afternoons. Tel: 01273 858337.

HAM HOUSE
London

BETWEEN RICHMOND AND KINGSTON-UPON-THAMES

Ham house is an outstanding Stuart house which has managed to avoid the changes in architectural fashion that have altered so many of its contemporaries over the years. It was built in 1610 on the south bank of the Thames in the days when the river was the major thoroughfare into the city, giving its owner, Knight Marshall of the King's Household to James, essential access to the royal households.

Some 60 years later the house was enlarged and redecorated in the most fashionable style by the Duke and Duchess of Lauderdale, and much of their work is evident today. Even some of the furniture, specially made for the house in the 17th century, remains in situ. It is likely that we have the Duchess of Lauderdale's extravagance to thank because she left her descendant decidedly short of any funds which might have been used to make alterations. Even when the family fortunes took an upturn, they seemed loath to spend any money on the house and by the time it came into the ownership of the National Trust much restoration was necessary.

Today the interior decoration is again sumptuous, with painted ceilings, gilded plasterwork and rich colours, and there is a particularly fine library. The garden is also being restored to its original design.

Open April to mid-December on selected afternoons. Tel: 0181-940 1950.

Ham House is an example of fine restoration work by the National Trust

Among the many special features of Hampton Court is the enclosed Royal (or Real) Tennis Court

HAMPTON COURT
London

1½ MILES (2 KM) WEST OF KINGSTON-UPON-THAMES

*The King's Court
Should have the excellence
But Hampton Court
Hath the pre-eminence*
John Skelton (poet)

In Tudor times, the quickest and easiest route into London from Hampton Court was by river. The great astronomical clock in the Clock Court enabled Henry VIII to determine the times of high and low tide at London Bridge.

Nearly 600 years of history are contained within this vast royal palace on the Thames. In the early 16th century the lease was acquired by Cardinal Wolsey, Henry VIII's chief minister, and he added most of the Tudor buildings that we see today. They included a complete range of apartments for the use of Henry VIII, Catherine of Aragon and Princess Mary. When the Cardinal fell from grace in the 1520s the palace was handed over to Henry as a placatory gesture and the King added the Great Hall, with its wonderful hammer-beam ceiling, and vast kitchens to cater for his 1,000-strong retinue. Later monarchs all left their mark, too.

There is so much to see at Hampton Court that six separate routes have been devised, each exploring a different theme: Henry VIII's magnificent state apartments; the Queen's apartments, built by Sir Christopher Wren for Queen Mary; the elegant Georgian rooms; the King's apartments, built by William III and restored following a dreadful fire in 1986; the Wolsey Rooms, the earliest of the Tudor Rooms which now house important Renaissance paintings; and the Tudor kitchens, which occupy over 50 rooms and are set up as if in preparation for a great Tudor banquet. Some sixty acres (24ha) of gardens include the famous maze and the Great Vine.

Open all year daily, except Christmas and New Year's Day. Tel: 0181-781 9500.

HATCHLANDS
Surrey

EAST CLANDON, 4 MILES (6.5 KM) EAST OF GUILDFORD

Musical visitors with suitable qualifications may arrange to play one of the pianos in the Cobbe Collection by contacting the house in advance.

When Alec Cobbe took the lease on Hatchlands in 1988 the house took on a new character which is entirely in keeping with its original purpose and style. With him he brought the Cobbe Collection of pictures, furniture and musical instruments that enliven the house today.

It is a house notable for many things, not least of which is the fact that the interior is the first documented work by Robert Adam, who came to dominate English architecture in the late 18th century. His fine ceilings and sculptured marble fireplaces are the chief glory of the house.

The arrival of Mr Cobbe heralded a programme of renovation and redecoration which is progressing beautifully, and the rooms are now bright and attractive, mostly furnished with Victorian pieces. Work is still in progress in the dining room, where hand-painted arabesque decoration is being undertaken by Edward Bulmer and by Alec Cobbe himself (by profession, a picture restorer, designer and artist). The fascinating collection of musical instruments, begun when Mr Cobbe was at university, concentrates on keyboard instruments – particularly harpsichords and forte-pianos – dating from 1750 to 1840, and there are plans to organise recitals by international artists.

Open from April to October on selected afternoons. Tel: 01483 222787.

The Adam interiors of Hatchlands are being brought back to life by the new owner

The splendid King James'
drawing room

HATFIELD HOUSE
Hertfordshire

HATFIELD, 18 MILES (29 KM) NORTH OF LONDON

Queen Elizabeth I's silk stockings are on display at Hatfield – they are possibly the first pair ever worn.

This impressive Tudor mansion has been the home of the Cecil family since James I swapped houses with Robert Cecil. Before that Hatfield was a royal residence, acquired by Henry VIII mainly for housing his children – each of whom came in turn to the throne before the Tudor dynasty was over. It was at Hatfield that Elizabeth I learned of her accession; her first act was to send for William Cecil, later Lord Burghley, and make him her Chief Minister. The enormous and distinctive mansion we see today is Jacobean, but part of the old palace remains and has been restored.

Hatfield House contains some fine works of art, including two portraits of Elizabeth I and one of Mary, Queen of Scots, said to have been painted just a few days before her execution. There are also some important tapestries and fine furniture in rooms as diverse as the immense, two-storeyed Marble Hall, with its oak panelling and minstrels' gallery, to the sumptuous King James' drawing room, essentially 18th-century in style and with a life-size statue of the king over the mantelpiece. The elaborately carved grand staircase is one of the finest examples in existence, and the armoury contains armour taken from the men of the Spanish Armada.

Open from Easter to mid-October on most afternoons. Tel: 01707 262823.

HEVER CASTLE
Kent

HEVER, 7 MILES (11.5 KM) WEST OF TONBRIDGE

Romance, intrigue, wealth, power and far-reaching decisions – all have been played out on the stage of Hever Castle. This was the childhood home of Anne Boleyn, for whom Henry VIII abandoned his wife, his faith and the faith of the nation. Anne's fate is well known, and her parents died, broken, within two years. Henry later gave Hever to his divorced wife Anne of Cleves. Over the centuries Hever went into a decline until, in 1903, it was bought by William Waldorf Astor who spent substantial amounts of his $100 million fortune on restoring the castle to its former magnificence.

Today Hever is as much a monument to early 20th-century craftsmanship as it is to the past. Room after room of splendid panelling and intricate carving blend perfectly with the original timbers. The rooms are furnished with antiques; walls are hung with splendid tapestries, one depicting Princess Mary's marriage to Louis XII of France, with Anne Boleyn reputedly among the attendants; portraits include a Holbein of Henry VIII, and Queen Elizabeth I by John Bettes the Younger. The dark and oppressive Henry VIII Room, with its great four-poster bed, is evocative of the period, but the most poignant is Anne Boleyn's Room, containing the prayer book she took with her to her execution.

Open from mid-March to October every afternoon. Tel: 01732 865224.

The restored Hever Castle proved too small for the Astors' lavish entertaining and the inspired solution was to build the 'Tudor Village'. This picturesque cluster of apparently individual cottages actually consists of 100 luxurious rooms, linked by corridors and a covered bridge over the moat to the castle.

A romantic castle, once the home of Anne Boleyn

The sumptuous Victorian mansion of Highclere

HIGHCLERE CASTLE
Hampshire

5 MILES (8 KM) SOUTH OF NEWBURY

The 5th Earl of Carnarvon was fascinated by archaeology as a child and later spent every winter in Egypt. Though he helped to discover the tomb of Tutankhamun, and even looked inside it, he died before he could look upon the ancient king – some say he was the victim of a curse on the tomb.

Whether seen from a distance, from the approach through the park or from close quarters, Highclere Castle cannot fail to impress. It is hardly surprising that its architect, Sir Charles Barry, preferred it to the other building he was working on at the time – the Houses of Parliament. Highclere is a great square, honey-coloured building with a central square tower and an intricate roofline.

Inside, the castle is just as impressive, with a series of magnificent rooms, each with its own charm and character, from the Gothic, fan-vaulted entrance hall to the delicate boudoir, Lady Carnarvon's private sitting room.

Among the most magnificent rooms are the saloon, also Gothic and two storeys high, with an open gallery and splendidly rich decoration, and the huge double library, styled after the Reform Club library in London. The main staircase fills the great square tower at the centre of the house, while the drawing room, lined with family portraits, is in rococo revival style.

Highclere is the home of the Earls of Carnarvon, and it was the 5th Earl who, with Howard Carter, discovered the tomb of Tutankhamun. There is a display of excavated finds in the cellars.

Open from July to September, afternoons, except Monday and Tuesday. Tel: 01635 253210.

KENSINGTON PALACE
London

KENSINGTON GARDENS, W8

*I*n 1689, William III, who suffered badly from asthma, bought what was then called Nottingham House, the country home of the Earl of Nottingham. He employed Sir Christopher Wren to remodel it and moved the royal household from Whitehall to the cleaner country air of Kensington.

The palace was enlarged and redecorated again for George I and was the principal private residence of the royal family until the death of George II. Queen Victoria was born here, and it was at Kensington Palace, in 1837, that she learned of her accession to the throne at the age of 17.

The palace is now the London home of several members of the royal family, including the Prince of Wales, Princess Margaret, and Prince and Princess Michael of Kent.

The state apartments, with rooms by Wren and William Kent, are furnished with pieces from the royal collection, and other rooms are sumptuously decorated in classical 18th-century style, with wonderful painted ceilings and fine works of art, including a large number of royal portraits. The palace is also the home of the Royal Ceremonial Dress Collection which contains some of the magnificent costumes worn at Court from 1750 onwards, including dresses worn by Queen Victoria at all stages of her life.

Open all year daily, except certain Bank Holidays. Tel: 0171-937 9561.

Kensington Palace was once considered a country residence

KINGSTON BAGPUIZE HOUSE
Oxfordshire

KINGSTON BAGPUIZE, 5 MILES (8 KM) WEST OF ABINGDON

Lady Tweedsmuir's father-in-law was the writer John Buchan, 1st Baron Tweedsmuir,. He wrote historical works as well as better-known adventure stories such as *The Thirty-nine Steps*.

No-one knows for certain when Kingston Bagpuize House was built, but it is thought to date from around 1670. It is a charming place, with a distinct 'lived-in' character.

One of its most important architectural features is the splendid cantilevered staircase, which has no supporting pillars. The pine-panelled hall and staircase have a Chinese theme, with hand-painted Chinese wallpapers and antique vases. The saloon is central to the whole design of the house – all the principal ground floor rooms can be seen from here, and the door into the garden was once the main entrance to the house. The further rooms are again panelled, with either oak or pine, and are beautifully furnished.

Originally the first floor had a great chamber, but this was divided up, probably in the early 18th century. The Rose Bedroom occupies some of this space, while the adjoining Lady Tweedsmuir's Bedroom would formerly have been the withdrawing room. Both have four-poster beds and fine Georgian furniture.

Today's visitors can take tea in the old kitchen, which has been very little changed to accommodate this facility, retaining its old dresser with kitchen china, a fine array of copper pans and a knife sharpener. The beautiful gardens were created by Miss Marnie Raphael, who lived here from 1939 to 1976 and was the aunt of Lady Tweedsmuir, the present owner.

Open for 30 days a year during the summer. Tel: 01865 820259.

This charming home has the perfect proportions of a doll's house

The elaborate Gothic banqueting hall

'You know very well that when the health, life and beauty now overflowing these halls shall have fled, crowds of people will come to see the place where he lived and wrote.'
Charles Dickens, making a speech in Knebworth's Banqueting Hall in which he referred to his friend and host Sir Edward Bulwer-Lytton

KNEBWORTH HOUSE
Hertfordshire

STEVENAGE, WITH DIRECT ACCESS OFF THE A1(M) AT JUNCTION 7

Successive owners of Knebworth House have been unable to resist wielding the hand of change. It was built by Sir Robert Lytton in 1490 and for about 300 years developed and grew until Mrs Elizabeth Bulwer-Lytton demolished a large part of it in 1810. It was her son, the Victorian author and playwright Sir Edward Bulwer-Lytton, who transformed the house into the vision of unrestrained High Gothic splendour we see today. It is theatrical and romantic, its roof line a mass of battlements, turrets and heraldic beasts.

Inside is a series of magnificent rooms – the banqueting hall, a fine example of 17th-century architecture; the elegant dining parlour; the richly decorated library; the ornately Victorian state drawing room; the charming Regency bedroom of Mrs Bulwer-Lytton and the Tudor-style Queen Elizabeth Room.

Bulwer-Lytton's study recalls the life and work of the author and there is an Indian exhibition – Robert, 1st Earl of Lytton was the Viceroy who proclaimed Queen Victoria Empress of India. All around are family portraits and photographs, and the Hampden Room contains the family collection of children's furniture, toys and books.

Open at Easter, and from June to August daily, except Monday, weekends and Bank Holidays in April, May and September. Tel: 01438 812661.

LAYER MARNEY TOWER
Essex

6 MILES (9.5 KM) SOUTH-WEST OF COLCHESTER

Layer Marney Tower, below, is a well-known East Anglian landmark, and the Long Gallery, right, was clearly conceived for entertaining on a grand scale

When Henry VIII was on the throne, his namesake Henry, 1st Lord Marney, began to build a new home for himself which would reflect his new-found wealth and importance. He was a valued and respected member of the Privy Council under both Henry VII and Henry VIII, and his sound advice earned him first a knighthood and then a baronetcy. Though his great Tudor mansion was never completed, it remains as impressive today as when it was first constructed.

Layer Marney Tower, one of East Anglia's great landmarks and the tallest Tudor gatehouse in the country, has exceptionally fine brickwork and splendid terracotta decoration featuring shells and dolphins crowning the corner towers. The use of terracotta was a very recent innovation at that time, showing that Henry was seriously interested in keeping up with the trends of the times. Though there are actually only three storeys to the gatehouse itself, the hexagonal corner towers rise high above the roofline and have eight layers of windows. Between the corner turrets lie two respectably-sized rooms which may well have been used as state apartments for visiting royalty. Sadly, Henry Marney died before the building could be finished and his son died just two years later, leaving no-one to realise the dream.

Since that time the Tower has had a succession of owners, but each has admirably cared for this remarkable building.

East and west wings spread out on either side of the tower and there is a completely isolated south wing, not joined to the rest of the building at all, but these wings are all private living quarters of the owners and it is only the gatehouse that is open to the public. Visitors can climb right up to the top for a close look at the fine architectural features, and for good views, and there are displays of documents relating to the history of the tower and the families who have lived there over the centuries.

Within the grounds is a farm centred on a medieval barn and still worked by traditional methods. A farm walk takes in the variety of animals which are kept. Most of them are rare breeds, including Red Poll cattle and Norfolk Horn sheep, and there is a farming exhibition. Layer Marney had a licence to enclose deer in a park in 1267, and today there are 200 red deer again on the farm.

Open from April to September every afternoon, except Saturday. Tel: 01206 330784.

This Victorian house has had a chequered history, and is now the headquarters of a religious sect

MENTMORE TOWERS
Buckinghamshire

6 MILES (9.5 KM) NORTH-EAST OF AYLESBURY

Mentmore Towers is certainly the kind of mansion one might expect to have been built for Baron Meyer Amschel de Rothschild at the height of the Victorian age of confidence and prosperity. It is a vast and splendid building in Elizabethan style, with huge windows and a many-turreted roofline, which was constructed in the mid-19th century to a design by Joseph Paxton and his future son-in-law, G H Stokes. Paxton was actually not a trained architect, but he was a great favourite of the Rothschild family, who were, perhaps, impressed by the Crystal Palace he had built for the Great Exhibition of 1851. Certainly, the building here makes great use of natural light.

Towards the end of the 19th century Mentmore became the home of Lord Rosebery, and was a glittering centre of social life for the wealthy and influential. It was also a veritable treasure-house of fine furniture and works of art and when, in the 1970s, the contents were put up for sale by auction there was a public outcry against the possible loss to the nation of important items. The auction went ahead, however, and raised over six million pounds in total. The building was subsequently purchased by the Maharishi Mahesh Yogi. It is still the headquarters of his University of Natural Law.

Open all year on Sunday and Bank Holiday afternoons. Tel: 01296 661881.

NETHER WINCHENDON
Buckinghamshire

LOWER WINCHENDON, 6 MILES (9.5 KM) SOUTH-WEST OF AYLESBURY

Rarely have 19th-century architectural additions blended so harmoniously with an ancient building as at Nether Winchendon, perhaps because the owner, Sir Scrope Bernard, was his own architect. No-one can say how much of the building dates back to 1162, when the property was granted to the nearby monastery of Notley, but some parts are clearly medieval and Tudor. The charming drawing room has pale oak linenfold panelling and a delicate frieze, thought to have been produced at the monastery in the 16th century. The Great Hall contains the only contemporary tapestry portrait of Henry VIII, part of an early Flemish work which may commemorate the king becoming Defender of the Faith. The Justice Room is panelled in walnut grown on the estate and the 19th-century entrance hall has some fascinating charters and other documents, including a summons to the Barebones Parliament of 1653, signed by Oliver Cromwell.

Since 1559, when it was bought by a London merchant, Nether Winchendon has changed hands only by inheritance and marriage, and for the last 200 years has been in the care of the Bernard family. Former Bernards have included a Governor of New Jersey and Massachusetts, a distinguished social reformer who campaigned for vaccination, cancer research and better conditions for children working in the mills.

Open May and August, Bank Holiday Sunday and Monday. Tel: 01844 290101.

Dark panelling warms the Great Hall

OSBORNE HOUSE
Isle of Wight

1 MILE (1.5 KM) SOUTH-EAST OF EAST COWES

'It is impossible to see a prettier place, with woods and valleys and points of view, which would be beautiful anywhere; but when these are combined with the sea (to which the woods grow down) and a beach which is quite private, it really is everything one could wish.'
Queen Victoria

Osborne was designed in the style of an Italianate villa, below, with right, matching terraces and gardens

Queen Victoria and Prince Albert, dissatisfied with the turmoil of life at Court and the general lack of privacy they had to endure, decided to seek out a peaceful holiday retreat which would be large and private enough for their needs. Recalling happy childhood holidays, Victoria turned her attention to the Isle of Wight and in 1844 the royal couple rented Osborne House for a year's trial period. Though the original house proved to be too small, its situation on rising ground overlooking the Solent delighted the Queen and her consort and they bought the house and its 1,000 acres (405ha) of land in 1845.

Prince Albert remarked that the view from Osborne reminded him of the Bay of Naples, and when he and his builder, Thomas Cubitt, drew up plans for a new house it took the form of a Neapolitan villa, with Italianate campaniles and a loggia. The Prince, as keen on science and industry as he was on architecture, employed a number of innovative construction methods, including the use of cast-iron beams.

Outside, Albert created mock Renaissance terraces, with statues and a fountain, reaching down to the sea where they had a private beach, and planted acres of trees on the surrounding estate. He also imported a Swiss chalet as a play house for the royal children, but it had an educational purpose too – the boys were taught carpentry, the princesses learned cooking and household management, and each of the children had a garden plot where they grew flowers and vegetables.

This idyllic place became Victoria's favourite home and she lived here for most of the time until she died (at Osborne) in 1901. When Prince Albert died from typhoid in 1861, the heart-broken queen issued instructions that

nothing at Osborne should be changed so that it would remain as a memorial to the man who had created it. Hardly anything has changed here since Queen Victoria died either, and there are many of her personal possessions, including her own and Prince Albert's paintings and gifts among the grand works of art and statues which adorn the state rooms.

In contrast to the Italian style, the Durbar Room, added in 1891 as a dining room and decorated in Indian style by Indian craftsmen, reflects the Queen's role as Empress of India.

Osborne is now not only a memorial to Prince Albert, but also to his remarkable Queen and to the Victorian age.

Open from April to October daily. Tel: 01983 200022.

In her memoirs Queen Victoria noted that she and Prince Albert would often walk in the woods at Osborne and that Albert would imitate the distinctive song of the nightingale, his favourite bird – frequently receiving a reply.

OSTERLEY PARK
London

1 MILE (1.5 KM) NORTH-EAST OF HOUNSLOW

*T*he area between Heathrow Airport and Chiswick hardly seems a likely location for a splendid mansion set in 140 acres (56ha) of parkland, but this is where you will find Osterley Park. The original house dates back to 1575 when it was built for Sir Thomas Gresham, founder of the Royal Exchange, but it is actually known today as one of the most complete examples of the work of Robert Adam. Between 1760 and 1780 Adam transformed the house into a superb neo-classical villa, with the intricate plasterwork for which he was famous. By this time, Osterley was owned by Robert Child, a very wealthy London banker.

The house is entered by a huge double portico, built between the two towers of the original building, and this leads into a magnificent entrance hall with Roman statues and stucco panels. The state apartments include an ornately decorated four-poster bed, an ante room with Gobelin tapestries and a dressing room decorated in the Etruscan style, its walls ornamented with classical figures and urns. Adam's involvement at Osterley did not stop at the house – he also built the semi-circular garden house within the landscaped grounds.

A fine reminder of earlier times can be seen in the stable block which remains largely unaltered from Gresham's original building.

Open from April to October on most afternoons. Tel: 0181-560 3918.

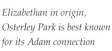

Elizabethan in origin, Osterley Park is best known for its Adam connection

PENSHURST PLACE
Kent

PENSHURST, 4½ MILES (7 KM) NORTH-WEST OF TUNBRIDGE WELLS

Penshurst Place represents an intriguing blend of architectural styles

The original part of Penshurst Place was built between 1340 and 1345 for Sir John de Pulteney, and although it was extended and modified by successive owners its magnificent baron's hall is superbly preserved. This was the heart of the medieval house, where the entire household lived beneath the wonderful chestnut-beamed roof; its central fireplace is still evident today. It is the oldest and the finest example of a medieval hall in the country.

Penshurst was closely connected with royalty, belonging at one time to Henry IV's third son, and later to Henry VIII. His son, Edward VI, gave the property to Sir William Sidney in 1552 and it is still the Sidney family home.

A great variety of architectural styles are incorporated in the building we see today, though its battlemented exterior presents a unified face, and its series of interesting rooms provides a splendid backdrop for the superb furniture, crystal chandeliers, tapestries and works of art. There are family portraits everywhere, including one of that famous ancestor, Sir Philip Sidney, the great Elizabethan soldier, courtier and poet. A tremendous amount of restoration work has been carried out since World War II, when Penshurst was damaged by flying bombs, and it is as much a monument to the most recent generations of Sidneys as to its great figures of the past.

Open from Easter to October every afternoon. Tel: 01892 870307.

POLESDEN LACEY
Surrey

3 MILES (5 KM) NORTH-WEST OF DORKING

*T*he previous house on this site was owned by the playwright Richard Brinsley Sheridan, but his only remaining legacy here is the long terraced walk, the most impressive feature of the garden. Two years after his death the property was sold to Joseph Bonsor, who commissioned the large, but pleasantly unpretentious house we see today.

Polesden Lacey really came into its own during the Edwardian era, when the estate belonged to the Hon Ronald Greville and his wife. Until the outbreak of World War II the house was alive with high society gatherings, presided over by the vivacious Mrs Greville. The daughter of the Right Hon William McEwan, one-time Member of Parliament and founder of the McEwan brewery, she was a charming but determined lady with high social ambitions. Through her husband's connections she found her way into the Marlborough House circle of Edward VII, and after her husband died in 1908 she capitalised on those introductions until she was a much sought-after hostess, entertaining the King and his friends on a lavish scale at Polesden Lacey. The Duke and Duchess of York (later George VI and Queen Elizabeth), spent part of their honeymoon here. The visitors' books, menus, photographs and newspaper cuttings which survive here are,

The rooms are beautifully furnished with family treasures, below, while right, terraced lawns sweep away from the house

perhaps, the most telling reminders of the high life they all enjoyed.

'Ronnie' Greville's enormous strength of character still permeates Polesden Lacey to this day, and her fine collections of paintings, tapestries, porcelain and other works of art furnish the house in handsome style. On her death in 1942 she bequeathed the house to the National Trust as a memorial to her father. She herself is buried in the grounds.

The interior of the house consists of a series of fascinating rooms ranged around a central courtyard; the entrance hall, two storeys high, is both welcoming and impressive. The dining room, scene of Mrs Greville's sumptuous dinner parties, has some beautiful silver and porcelain, and the drawing room has carved and gilt panelling that may have come from an Italian palace. Most of the art collection is displayed in the corridor around the courtyard, and includes the work of Italian and Dutch artists.

In keeping both with its literary origins and the era of great social gatherings, Polesden Lacey now stages an open-air theatre season during the summer.

Open most afternoons from April to October; weekends only during March and November. Tel: 01372 458203 or 452048.

Standen is a charming tribute to the Arts and Crafts movement of the 19th century

STANDEN
West Sussex

1½ MILES (2 KM) SOUTH OF EAST GRINSTEAD

*T*his delightful house was built between 1891 and 1894 by Philip Webb for the Beale family and is a showpiece of the 19th-century Arts and Crafts movement. Webb, along with William Morris, was a leading light in the movement, whose main principles concerned the promotion of craftsmanship as opposed to the mass-production of the Victorian age. Generally the architect would specify not only the building design but also the interior fittings and furniture, and Standen has some beautifully preserved William Morris wallpapers and fabrics. His designs here include the famous Sunflower, Peacock, Trellis and Larkspur motifs, among others.

The furniture was also custom made and includes contemporary brass beds from Heal's, furniture from the Morris company and ceramics by William de Morgan. Webb himself designed some of the furniture, as well as such details as the fire grates, the electric light fittings and the finger-plates for the doors.

Standen is a rambling house which looks for all the world as if it had developed over many centuries, rather than having been completed in a relatively short space of time, and this is due to Webb's use of the vernacular style and traditional building materials.

Open most afternoons from April to October and weekends in March. Tel: 01342 323029.

STANTON HARCOURT MANOR
Oxfordshire

STANTON HARCOURT, 5 MILES (8 KM) SOUTH-EAST OF WITNEY

Pope's Tower commemorates the period 1717–18 when it was lent to Alexander Pope as a place where he could work on his translation of The Iliad. Scratched onto a window pane are the words, 'In the year 1718 I, Alexander Pope, finished here the fifth volume of Homer.'

Set in a picturesque and historic village, Stanton Harcourt Manor is a fine example of an early medieval unfortified manor house. It came to the Harcourt family upon the marriage of Robert de Harcourt to Isabel de Cambille in the middle of the 12th century. The bride's mother was a cousin of Queen Adeliza, the second wife of Henry I, and the Queen gave the couple the Lordship of Stanton as a wedding gift.

The house has seen many ups and downs over the centuries, and for some time was abandoned and neglected, but now, over eight centuries later, the Harcourt family once again live here. Originally built between 1380 and 1470 around three sides of a square, the western side housed the Great Kitchen, along with servants' quarters and offices, and this is still standing. The eastern wing, however, has completely disappeared and only one corner – Pope's Tower – remains of the north side. On the ground floor of the tower is the chapel, with a fan-vaulted chancel roof and a wooden nave ceiling, still used by the family and parishioners. The Great Kitchen, one of the earliest parts of the house, is unique: its unusual conical roof was designed to let out smoke from the cooking fires.

Open from April to September on selected days. Tel: 01865 881928.

The portrait over the fireplace in the dining room is of Lettice, wife of the 4th Lord Paget

*The mellow golden stonework
of Stratfield Saye*

STRATFIELD SAYE
Hampshire

6 MILES (9.5 KM) SOUTH OF READING

The Duke's charger, Copenhagen, was buried in the Ice House paddock where his grave is marked with a headstone and a turkey oak, grown from an acorn planted at the time of his burial.

*A*fter the Battle of Waterloo the first Duke of Wellington returned home a hero, and a grateful nation voted to grant him £600,000 with which to provide himself with a grand country house. He bought the estate at Stratfield Saye mainly for the parkland, for it was his intention to build a splendid new palace in the north-eastern corner.

Sadly, the grandiose plans for a palace to rival Blenheim far out-stripped the joint funds of the national gift and his personal wealth.

Pragmatically, the Duke decided to settle for what he had, and set about modernising what was considered to be a modest house for so great a man. Among other improvements he installed blue patterned china water closets in every room and a central heating system – an unheard of luxury, and one which prompted Queen Victoria to complain that it was too hot. One of the original radiators can be seen in the staircase hall.

The main part of the house was built around 1630, and later additions,

including the conservatory and the two outer wings, have been carefully blended with the existing architecture.

If any room can be said to reflect its owner then it is the Hall, with its dignified, essentially masculine character and an array of items recalling Wellington's triumphs. There are paintings of events at Waterloo and the Peninsular War, busts of Wellington and Napoleon, and relics of the Duke's funeral.

The library has changed little since the 1st Duke's day and the music room is now dedicated to the memory of his favourite charger, Copenhagen, who carried him all day at the Battle of Waterloo. There are a number of paintings of the horse here and a bronze of Wellington mounted on him.

The tour of the house takes in many rooms, including the beautiful gallery, decorated in gold leaf, where there is a series of classical bronze busts. The charming 'small' drawing room, with French wallpaper, has a collection of miniatures, drawings and paintings, including a delightful study of the Duke and his grandchildren. The drawing room is a riot of green and gold with gilded plasterwork and Chippendale mirrors.

An exhibition on the life and times of the Duke of Wellington can be found in part of the stable block. This includes a special display relating to his state funeral, when a massive funeral carriage pulled by twelve dray horses was to process through London. In the event, the heavy carriage proved extremely difficult to manoevre.

Open from May to September daily, except Friday. Tel: 01256 882882.

STONOR HOUSE
Oxfordshire

4½ MILES (7 KM) NORTH OF HENLEY-ON-THAMES

The Stonor family have lived in this pleasant spot in the Chiltern Hills for at least 800 years, and their delightful home has developed over the centuries from the original medieval house which remains at its heart to the red-brick Georgian mansion we see today.

It is a very interesting house, with fine, well-proportioned rooms. The dining room still has its early 19th-century French wallpaper showing important buildings of Paris arranged next to one another along the River Seine. The study has an excellent collection of Italian drawings and a pair of rare Venetian globes, while Francis Stonor's Bedroom has a curious shell-shaped bed and shell chairs. Mortlake tapes-tries hang in the Long Gallery, along with family portraits, and the Edmund Campion Room has displays relating to Father Edmund Campion, who lost his life for his Catholic faith in 1581.

Beside the house is the chapel, where Mass has been celebrated continuously since 1349, even through the years of Catholic suppression. The Stonors have always been a devout family, and a large number of them have entered religious life. Though it is a private chapel, many local Catholics attend Mass there.

The lovely grounds include a re-creation of the stone circle which once stood on the site.

Open from April to September on selected afternoons. Tel: 01491 638587.

The private chapel is an important feature of Stonor House

The stunning double colonnade

WEST WYCOMBE HOUSE
Buckinghamshire

3 MILES (5 KM) WEST OF HIGH WYCOMBE

Successive generations of Dashwoods have been trying to live down the exploits of the second Sir Francis who gained notoriety as a member of the Hell Fire Club. It is carefully pointed out these days that he was also Postmaster General from 1766 to 1781, a Fellow of the Royal Society and of the Society of Antiquaries, and a founder member of the Dilettanti Society. The second Sir Francis was also responsible for the transformation of West Wycombe House (built by his predecessor), continuing to make improvements until his death in 1781.

West Wycombe remains much as the second Sir Francis left it, and is acknowledged as an important monument to neo-classicism. Behind the façades, which include a double colonnade on the south front and a splendid Ionic portico on the west, are a series of rooms which continue the classical theme. The hall and staircase have been likened to a Roman atrium, the painted ceiling of the saloon represents the Council of the Gods, and that in the Blue Drawing Room, formerly the dining room, depicts the Triumph of Bacchus and Ariadne. Here also is a copy of the Venus de Medici. Much of the decoration is very rare, and is complemented with fine paintings and tapestries.

Open June to August afternoons, except Thursday and Friday. Tel: 01494 524411.

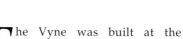

THE VYNE
Hampshire

SHERBORNE ST JOHN, 4 MILES (6.5 KM) NORTH OF BASINGSTOKE

*T*he Vyne was built at the beginning of the 16th century by William Sandys, a loyal and discreet member of Henry VIII's court who rose to become Lord Chamberlain and entertained the King on several occasions at his Hampshire home. Elizabeth I was also a visitor, but during the Civil War it was Parliamentarians rather than Royalists who assembled there. That struggle considerably reduced the Sandys fortune, so that the 6th Lord Sandys found it necessary to sell the house and retire to his other home – Mottisfont Abbey.

Below, wide lawns stretch down to the lake, and right, the magnificent classical staircase is not to be missed

The new owner was Chaloner Chute, a prosperous barrister with a reputation as an unbiased and just advocate, who had managed to avoid politics during the Civil War, but later became a Member of Parliament and Speaker of the House. He made various improvements to The Vyne before his death in 1659. His grandson, Edward, was responsible for the collection of fine Queen Anne furniture and Soho tapestries which can now be seen in the house.

Another Chute to leave his mark on the house was Edward's son, John,

who, after an initial reluctance to inherit The Vyne at all, designed for it a spectacular classical-style staircase hall. John was a great friend of Horace Walpole, and the Strawberry Parlour is not only named after Walpole's house, Strawberry Hill, but was also reserved for his use whenever he visited his friend here. Walpole certainly offered his advice on what should be done with The Vyne, and this charming little room contains prints and drawings which relate to the two friends.

On the ground floor of the house, the stone gallery occupies the whole of the west wing and contains a series of busts and statues. From here a series of rooms stretches along the north side of the house, including the 'further' drawing room with its delicate plaster ceiling , the ante room, where a fine collection of china and porcelain is on display, and the 'large' drawing room, where a carved fire-

place is painted to resemble stone. The dining room still has its Elizabethan wood panelling and a charming pair of paintings by Sebastian Pether entitled *Sunrise* and *Moonlight*.

Beyond the chapel parlour and the ante-chapel is the chapel itself, one of the most perfect private chapels in the country. It has a screen that came from Windsor Castle, intricate carvings and a fine trio of late-Gothic windows. The adjacent tomb chamber was built by John Chute in about 1770 as a memorial to his ancestor, Chaloner Chute.

Open April to September afternoons, except Monday and Friday, but open on Bank Holidays. Tel: 01256 881337.

Even in its works of art, Calke Abbey breaks the mould. Rather than having the usual Print Room, as in other historic houses, the Harpurs favoured a collection of satirical caricatures on political and society themes, representing the finest exponents of the art form of their day.

CALKE ABBEY
Derbyshire

TICKNALL, 8 MILES (13 KM) SOUTH OF DERBY

Calke Abbey is now in the charge of the National Trust

Calke Abbey is, perhaps, one of the few places which can rightly claim to be unique. It is certainly different from the usual stately home, and this is largely due to the family who occupied it for more than 300 years. A former Augustinian abbey was an appropriate choice of home for the Harpurs, who were noted for their reclusive tendencies. With a sizeable fortune made in Elizabethan times from the law, the Harpurs lavished a great deal of money on updating the Tudor house, first in baroque style, later in neo-classical style.

It was Sir Henry Harpur (1763-1819) who compounded the reclusive label which still attaches to his family name. He somewhat pretentiously adopted the name of the Crewe barons, distant relations by marriage, and renamed his home – but then spoilt the whole effect by marrying a lady's maid, and was ostracised by his contemporaries.

His great-grandson was another character. Sir Vauncey Harpur Crewe had an overriding passion for natural history, to the extent of hanging hunting trophies over his bed. His collection of stuffed creatures, birds' eggs, shells and walking sticks add to the eccentricities to be found around the house.

The National Trust, which acquired the property in 1985, have managed to carry out essential repairs to the house while retaining its 'time capsule' appearance.

Open April to October afternoons, except Thursday and Friday. Tel: 01332 863822.

CHARLECOTE PARK
Warwickshire

3 MILES (5 KM) EAST OF STRATFORD-UPON-AVON

Surrounded by deer-park, the house backs delightfully on to the river

An imposing two-storey Elizabethan gateway, complete with balustrading and corner towers topped by cupolas, is a more than suitable introduction to the beautiful 16th-century home of the Lucy family. They came to this country with William the Conqueror, and Charlecote has been the family home since the 12th century, although the present house was built around 1551. It still looks Elizabethan, but this is largely due to 19th-century nostalgia for days gone by. George Hammond Lucy, who inherited the house in 1823, swept away all the changes that the intervening generations had made and recreated the original style in consultation with an antiquarian specialist.

The Great Hall is particularly convincing, though its barrel-vaulted ceiling is plaster painted to look like timber, and the hall is now a superb showcase for family portraits. The largest, hung above the fireplace, is a delightful representation of Sir Thomas Lucy III and his family.

Elsewhere there are ornamented plaster ceilings above richly coloured wallpaper and wood panelling, magnificent pieces of furniture – the most startling must be the hugely ornate bed in the Ebony Bedroom, which was made from a 17th-century East Indian settee – and fine works of art. In contrast, the range of domestic buildings includes the kitchen, scullery, laundry, brewhouse and a coach house, still with a collection of family coaches.

Open from April to October daily, except Wednesday and Thursday. Tel: 01789 470277.

A popular story has it that Shakespeare was apprehended for poaching deer in the park at Charlecote and that this was the reason for his quick departure to London – where, of course, he found fame and fortune.

Above and right, nestling in the lovely Derwent Valley, Chatsworth is the epitome of a stately home

CHATSWORTH
Derbyshire

1.5 MILES (2 KM) SOUTH OF BAKEWELL

In 1939 a girls' school was relocated to Chatsworth. Assemblies were held in the painted hall, physics were taught in the butler's pantry, art in the orangery, biology in the still room and chemistry out of harm's way in the stable block. There were dormitories all round the house, and 20 girls slept in the state drawing room.

*T*his palatial home of the Dukes of Devonshire, which sits splendidly in the Derwent Valley, is one of the grandest and best-loved of all the stately homes in Britain. The first house at Chatsworth was built by Bess of Hardwick, Countess of Shrewsbury, a remarkable lady who had four husbands and grew substantially richer and more powerful with each widowhood. At Chatsworth she was with her second husband, Sir William Cavendish, and they began building here in 1552, though the development of the house continued over many years.

In 1686 the 4th Earl, who was created 1st Duke of Devonshire in 1694, began to demolish parts of it to make way for new buildings designed by Thomas Archer. He also rebuilt the west front and lived just long enough to see completed the supremely beautiful house which delights visitors today. Only the chapel, the state dining room and the sculpture gallery remained as they were originally built.

Marble statuary from the 1st century AD in the north entrance hall and the painted ceiling panel provide a hint of the glories to come, but few visitors are prepared for the breathtaking painted

hall, with the whole of the ceiling and upper walls covered with scenes from the life of Julius Caesar, painted by Louis Laguerre in 1692. Amidst all this splendour, the children's Christmas party takes place every year, and the knowledge of this adds a delightful human touch to the beautiful but inanimate features.

The series of state rooms continues in equally grand style, suitably furnished and adorned with fine works of art and magnificent Mortlake tapestries. In the state music room there is also a touch of humour in the form of a *trompe-l'oeil* painting of a violin on an inner door which really does deceive the eye, even at very close quarters.

The bed in the state bedroom originally belonged to King George II, and on his death it was presented to the 4th Duke. King George V and Queen Mary slept here when they stayed at Chatsworth for the Royal Show at Derby in 1933.

The Oak Room is the oldest room in the house, with oak panelling and carved heads from a German monastery, one of the many purchases made by the 6th Duke. An avid collector of art and classical works, he was just one in a long line of Cavendishes who have shaped this splendid house and filled it with wonderful things.

Open from late March to October daily. Tel: 01246 582204.

DODDINGTON HALL
Lincolnshire

3 MILES (5 KM) SOUTH OF LINCOLN

George Jarvis was the Garrison Brigade Major at Dover Castle at the time when French Napoleonic prisoners of war were incarcerated there. He bought no less than three elaborate chess sets made by the prisoners from turned mutton bone, demonstrating, perhaps, a streak of sympathy for the men, as this was their sole source of income.

Below and right, from the outside Doddington Hall betrays its Elizabethan pedigree, but inside, 18th-century elegance prevails

Doddington House has the distinction of never having been sold, but it has passed by marriage through four families – the Tailors, the Husseys, the Delavels and finally the Jarvises, who are the present occupants. It was originally built for Thomas Tailor by the Elizabethan architect, Robert Smithson.

The white hall, which was the Great Hall in Elizabethan times, is still used on special occasions as a dining room; it is overlooked by portraits of ancestors of the Hussey and Delavel families. Rare gilt *carton pierre* ornaments and gilt mirror frames, bought by John Delavel in 1775, adorn the drawing room, a staggering 52ft (15.8m) in length, which appears today just as it did in the 18th century. In Elizabethan times the Long Gallery had windows along both sides and was used by the family for exercise and recreation. According to records, in 1756 that exercise would have included its use as a bowling alley!

More stately pleasures ensued in the 1760s when John Delavel turned it into a picture gallery. His interest in art may well have been fuelled by the family friendship with Sir Joshua Reynolds, who painted the full-length portrait of Sir Francis Delavel which hangs at the foot of the front stairs; they were an artistic family in any case – two small paintings of Seaton Delavel, the principal family home of the Delavels, painted by Edward

Hussey Delavel, may be seen above a cabinet at the top of the stairs.

The artistic bent continued into the Jarvis family, and the Print Room commemorates the life and work of George Ralph Payne Jarvis, the first member of his family to live at Doddington and a man of many talents. A solicitor by profession, he was also an accomplished artist and woodcarver, as examples of his work on display at Doddington show.

In the Tiger Room is a magnificent four-poster bed with crimson hangings of Spitalfields silk, which had to be transported to Doddington Hall by sea. The walls are hung with beautiful Flemish tapestries brought here from other rooms around the house. Several portraits, including one of Thomas Tailor, the son of the builder of Doddington Hall, decorate the oak panelled walls of the parlour, preserved in its original Queen Anne style.

Extensive parkland surrounds the Hall and there is a delightful walled rose garden.

Open from May to September on selected days. Tel: 01522 694308.

Elton Hall boasts a fine and extensive garden, carefully restored by the current owners

❖
ELTON HALL
Cambridgeshire

8 MILES (13 KM) WEST OF PETERBOROUGH
❖

*O*ver the years the vagaries of architectural fashion have left their mark on Elton Hall, which resembles a cross between a monastic foundation and a fairy-tale castle. This, however, bears witness to the Gothic revival of the late 18th to early 19th centuries, but that is not to say that Elton is not truly historic, for the earliest part dates back to the 15th century.

Inside, Elton Hall is 18th-century through and through, with its elegant Marble Hall and the sumptuous, richly decorated state dining room which doubles as a picture gallery. For over 300 years, since Sir Peter Proby was granted land and property at Elton by Queen Elizabeth I, this has been the home of the Proby family and successive generations have demonstrated excellent taste in their acquisition of fine works of art.

Each room offers a new delight, including Old Masters, pre-Raphaelite paintings and works by such great British artists as Gainsborough, Constable and Reynolds. The state drawing room is a vision of gold and cream, with delicately decorated plasterwork, gilt-framed portraits, and a huge mirror above the fireplace contrasting with the charming family photographs. The library, believed to be one of the finest still in private hands, retains an exceptional ecclesiastic section which includes Henry VIII's prayer book, inscribed by the monarch and two of his wives.

Open from May to August on selected days. Tel: 01832 280223.

HARDWICK HALL
Derbyshire

4½ MILES (7 KM) NORTH-WEST OF MANSFIELD

Elizabeth, Countess of Shrewsbury – 'Bess of Hardwick' – was a remarkable and very shrewd woman. She came from a fairly modest background and proceeded to outlive four husbands, each richer and higher on the social strata than the one that went before. With her wealth, Bess built great houses, including Chatsworth, but Hardwick Hall was the last, begun when she was 70 after the death of her fourth husband, the Earl of Shrewsbury, in 1590.

With architect Robert Smythson she created an impressive mansion with enormous windows and six great towers surmounted by her ornately fashioned monogram – ES. Inside, the Hall was designed specifically to house the collection of tapestries which still line its walls, and the Long Gallery, running the length of the east front, is hung with family portraits.

When Bess died in 1608 Hardwick passed to William Cavendish who bought his brother's share in Chatsworth and made this the principal family seat. Thus Hardwick Hall was left quite unaltered by succeeding generations.

As well as being a splendid example of its age, Hardwick has some particularly important works of embroidery, some worked by Bess herself, others by Mary, Queen of Scots, who was confined here for a time. The sumptuous embroidery of the bedhead in the state bedroom is an outstanding example.

Open from April to October on selected afternoons. Tel: 01246 850430.

Magnificent tapestries adorn the walls of the Blue Bedroom

Thomas William Coke was a fervent supporter of the Americans during the War of Independence, and each evening he is said to have toasted George Washington as the 'greatest man on this earth'.

'An Englishman's home is his castle.'
First said by Sir Edward Coke

HOLKHAM HALL
Norfolk

2 MILES (3 KM) WEST OF WELLS-NEXT-THE-SEA

The Coke (pronounced 'Cook') family were established at Holkham long before the present Palladian mansion was built. Their ancestor, Sir Edward Coke, was Attorney General to Elizabeth I and Chief Justice to James I, and his home was an Elizabethan manor house. When his descendant, Thomas Coke, returned from a six-year Grand Tour he realised that the manor was too small to accommodate the immense collections of works of art that he had accumulated. He had the house demolished and in 1743 a fine new classical-style Holkham Hall began to take shape which would suit his acquisitions.

The Marble Hall is modelled on a Roman Temple of Justice, and in the north dining room, tablets on the chimneypieces depict two of Aesop's Fables, *The Bear and the Beehive* and *The Sow with her Litter and the Wolf*. The state gallery has a superb collection of classical sculpture, including a statue of Diana and a bust of Thucydides which date back to about 4BC.

Perhaps the most famous member of the family is Thomas William Coke, better known as 'Coke of Norfolk'. A patron of agricultural inventions, and Member of Parliament for Norfolk, he was also responsible for the planting of no less than a million trees at Holkham.

Open from June to September daily, except Friday and Saturday. Tel: 01328 710227.

Holkham is one of the greatest 18th-century houses in England

*The central rotunda of
Ickworth is unmistakable*

ICKWORTH
Suffolk

2½ MILES (4 KM) SOUTH OF BURY ST EDMUNDS

*E*ven amidst all the excesses of the 18th century the design of Ickworth was unusual, with its great oval rotunda at the centre and two large wings curving out on each side. The brainchild of Frederick Hervey, the 4th Earl of Bristol and Bishop of Derry, it was designed to house his collections of art and other items, but sadly he did not live to see his creation completed; the finishing touches were not made until 27 years after his death. It is quite obvious, even from first sight of the building today, that it was intended first and foremost as a gallery, with any domestic requirements taking second place.

The Earl Bishop's descendants may often have felt that they had been left with something of a white elephant, but they completed the house and made what alterations they could to create a more practical place to live. Ickworth's virtue as a showcase for the family's superb art collections, however, has always been undisputed.

The house is filled with treasures: paintings by Velasquez, Lawrence, Kauffmann, Gainsborough and others; fine furniture and porcelain and one of the most splendid collections of silver in the country. Some of the décor itself is an art form, as in the wonderful Pompeian Room.

Open from Easter to October on selected afternoons. Tel: 01284 735270.

Sir Nathanial Curzon had a passion for naval affairs and frequently conducted mock battles on the lake, with frigates manned by estate workers.

KEDLESTON HALL
Derbyshire

5 MILES (8 KM) NORTH-WEST OF DERBY

*M*any grand mansions claim to be the finest example of the work of the brilliant Scottish architect, Robert Adam, but Kedleston Hall is well up in the running. Its planning began, however, as something of a muddle. Sir Nathanial Curzon, who inherited the estate in 1758, accepted a design submitted by Matthew Brettingham and James Paine, and they had already built the pavilions and started on the ground floor of the main house when, in December 1758, Curzon was introduced to Robert Adam. He was so impressed by Adam's ideas that he gave him the job of directing the work of Kedleston Hall.

The entrance front has been described as the grandest Palladian façade in Britain; at its centre there is a vast Corinthian portico set on a high base with flights of steps on either side.

The interiors are no less impressive, and the first introduction is the magnificent Marble Hall, modelled on the ancient atrium of the classic Roman villa. The drawing room has a nautical theme, from the decorative plaster ceiling of grotesque sea creatures to the gilt settees carved with mermaids, tritons and dolphins. All around the house are fine works of art, including Old Masters, family portraits and superb furniture.

The Indian Museum displays the collection of one Lord Curzon's time as Viceroy of India.

Open from April to October daily, except Monday and Tuesday, but open for Bank Holiday Mondays. Tel: 01332 842191.

Kedleston was the home of the Curzons for over 800 years

KENTWELL HALL
Suffolk

LONG MELFORD, 3 MILES (5 KM) NORTH OF SUDBURY

Kentwell Hall is still a very much lived-in home

A long avenue of lime trees leads to this moated Elizabethan manor house of mellow red brick. The setting is perfect and the Hall is beautiful, but the real charm of Kentwell comes from the infectious enthusiasm of its current owners, Patrick and Judith Phillips, who have thrown themselves wholeheartedly into the continuing process of restoration.

Much of the work they have done with their own hands – frequently in the rather piecemeal way we might tackle our own homes, depending upon the mood of the moment – and the overall effect is delightful. There is usually some restoration work in progress, and that which is complete is impressive indeed. Leaded lights have replaced the Georgian sash windows, vast fireplaces have been opened up, partitions have been removed to reveal the original size of some of the rooms, and Tudor brickwork has been exposed, not to mention the extensive structural repairs that were necessary.

Pieces of fine 16th-century oak panelling were collected from all round the house and assembled in what is now called the Panelled Room, and a staircase was formed to give access to the splendid minstrels' gallery in the Great Hall. Here, and in the billiards room, are some fine examples of 15th- and 16th-century painted or stained glass.

Open from late July to September daily, also on selected days from late March to July. Tel: 01787 310207.

For two weeks in the summer and at holiday weekends the Tudor era really does come to life at Kentwell, when volunteers don the costume of the age and re-create life as it would have been lived at Kentwell, both for the gentry and their visitors and servants.

MELBOURNE HALL
Derbyshire

MELBOURNE, 9 MILES (14.5 KM) SOUTH OF DERBY

A fine, elegant mansion standing in celebrated grounds and gardens, Melbourne Hall has had a chequered history which goes back to the 12th century. Originally the residence of the Bishops of Carlisle, it was later committed to the hands of a succession of lessees who sadly neglected the building. By the time Sir Francis Needham purchased the lease he found it necessary to demolish and rebuild a large part of the Hall, thus creating the grand house which exists today.

Sir John Coke was the next owner and his descendant, Lord Ralph Kerr, and his family are still at Melbourne, providing the warm and comfortable lived-in atmosphere which so delights visitors. The house is beautifully furnished and contains many fine works of art.

There are some notable characters associated with the history of Melbourne -- mostly from the Lamb family, who became Lords Melbourne – with stories of doubtful parentage and moral lassitude. Lady Caroline Lamb, wife of the 2nd Viscount Melbourne, had a famous affair with Lord Byron which led to formal separation from her husband in 1825. The 2nd Viscount was to become Queen Victoria's first Prime Minister; he also gave his name to the Australian city. Another Victorian Prime Minister later owned Melbourne – Lord Palmerston, who was married to Emily Lamb.

Open daily during August. Tel: 01332 862502.

The gardens of Melbourne Hall were laid out in the 18th century in the style of Le Nôtre

*The beautiful, moated
Otley Hall*

OTLEY HALL
Suffolk

7 MILES (11.5 KM) NORTH OF IPSWICH

*I*t would seem that this exquisite moated hall, which dates from the 15th century, has not always received the loving care and attention that must surely be its due. Built by the Gosnold family, who occupied it for some 250 years, it was then sold to the Rebows who let it on a lease for the next 200 years. Although this action prevented the kind of 'modernising' that freehold owners are likely to have carried out, the building was sadly neglected.

Just before World War I, however, a saviour came along in the shape of Mrs Arthur Sherston, who carried out much restoration work, remodelled the east wing and modernised the kitchen and the main block. After her death the Hall was unoccupied again for a time while difficulties with the inheritance were sorted out, and it soon fell into another period of decline.

Since 1950 successive owners have done much to restore the house and gardens and the present owner, John Mosesson, is continuing this worthwhile task. Richly carved beams, herringbone brickwork and decorative plasterwork are in abundance throughout the house, the oldest part of which is the south wing. There is some lovely linenfold panelling in the parlour, with mullioned windows in the Great Hall and splendid wall paintings in the banquet hall.

Open on selected days in spring and summer. Tel: 01473 890264.

Narrowly rescued from demolition, Oxburgh owes its continued existence to a persistent Lady Bedingfeld

OXBURGH HALL
Norfolk

OXBOROUGH, 7 MILES (11.5 KM) SOUTH-WEST OF SWAFFHAM

*O*xburgh Hall has its roots firmly in the medieval era. Built for the Bedingfeld family in 1482, it has mellow stone walls rising sheer from the waters of its moat, and a great Tudor gatehouse. But Oxburgh's history is not only a long one, it has also experienced moments of danger and excitement. The fact that the house has survived at all is, indeed, little short of miraculous.

After the Civil War it was ransacked by Cromwell's men who set fire to part of it. Much later, in 1951, financial difficulties beset the family and after 500 years of the Bedingfeld family's occupation Oxburgh Hall was sold to a development company. Three months later that company put it up for auction, with the only prospective buyer being a demolition firm. However, at the eleventh hour, on the morning of the sale, Lady Bedingfeld raised enough money to make a successful bid and bought the house back.

There are portraits of the Bedingfeld family throughout the house, and the wonderful 17th-century wall-coverings of embossed and painted Spanish leather on the corridor and stairs are a notable feature. The King's Room, named in honour of a visit by Henry VII in 1497, now contains wall hangings embroidered by Mary, Queen of Scots and Elizabeth, Countess of Shrewsbury.

Open from late March to October on selected days. Tel: 01366 328258.

PECKOVER HOUSE
Cambridgeshire

WISBECH, 12 MILES (19 KM) SOUTH-WEST OF KING'S LYNN

*T*his elegant Georgian house dates back to 1722, when it was owned by the Southwell family. It was then bought by Jonathon Peckover, who ran a bank in one wing (part of the group that later formed Barclays Bank), but this part of the house was later demolished. The house, without its contents, was given to the National Trust in 1943. Coincidentally, Octavia Hill, who was a co-founder of the Trust, was born near by and the dressing room contains a small exhibition relating to her, as well as documents and photographs belonging to the Peckover family.

Although the original contents of the house were not included in the gift to the Trust, there are a number of reminders of the family in the form of watercolours painted by Peckovers and a number of family portraits. Otherwise, the house has been completely refurnished by the Trust, including a pair of Chinese Chippendale silver tables in the elegant blue and white drawing room, an early 19th-century mahogany secretaire at the foot of the staircase, and the pictures and prints – mainly of Wisbech and the surrounding area – on the walls of the breakfast room.

The lovely two-acre gardens include a recently restored reed barn.

Open from late March to October on selected afternoons. Tel: 01945 583463.

Orange trees in the glass houses of this elegant Georgian mansion are still bearing fruit, some 250 years after they were planted

Fine plasterwork adorns the ceiling of the Long Gallery

SUDBURY HALL
Derbyshire

SUDBURY, 6 MILES (9.5 KM) EAST OF UTTOXETER

In the early 17th-century, before the present Hall was built, a long and bitter family feud arose over the ownership of the Sudbury estate. The dispute was eventually settled, after protracted and expensive litigation, and it was agreed that the two opposing claimants should marry and live there together.

*U*sing the finest master-craftsmen and artists of the time, Lord George Vernon began this fine country house in 1664. With its unusual diapered brickwork, carved two-storey stone frontispiece, a cupola and a large number of tall chimneys, it is among the most important survivors of its age. The interior has splendid decorative plasterwork, ceiling paintings by Louis Laguerre, woodcarving by that supremo of the craft, Grinling Gibbons, and one of the finest staircases in any British country house.

Both outside and in, Sudbury Hall is ornate in the extreme and displays a number of architectural influences, including Jacobean and classical styles.

Successive generations of the Vernons often seriously considered alterations to the Hall, but few were ever carried out and it remains very much as it was originally intended to be.

The only major addition, in the 19th century, was a sympathetically designed service wing, and this now houses the National Trust Museum of Childhood. Children's life from the 18th century onwards is depicted here, but the main emphasis is on the Victorian and Edwardian periods. There is a wonderful collection of toys and dolls and, to illustrate the other side of the coin, there are 'chimney climbs' for adventurous would-be sweeps.

Open from April to September on selected afternoons. Tel: 01283 585305.

SULGRAVE MANOR
Northamptonshire

6 MILES (9.5 KM) NORTH-EAST OF BANBURY

*I*n 1914, just as the Great War was beginning, Sulgrave Manor was set up as a memorial to mark 100 years of peace between Britain and America. Sulgrave was the obvious choice – the ancestral home of George Washington, the first President of the United States of America. It was also in need of restoration, and funds were raised on both sides of the Atlantic to finance the operation. Many items relating to George Washington are now on display in the house, including his velvet coat, saddle bags, a lock of his hair, various documents and portraits.

One of the most interesting aspects of the exterior of the house is the Washington coat of arms above the main porch, its motif of mullets (stars) and bars (stripes) not surprisingly held to be the inspiration for the American Flag.

The first Washington to live here was Lawrence, Mayor of Northampton, who purchased the manor in 1539. It was his grandson, John, who emigrated to Virginia and became the great-grandfather of the first President.

George Washington memorabilia aside, Sulgrave is a fascinating house to visit, with some wonderful old pieces of furniture, and is all the more charming for its modest proportions.

Open from April to October daily, except Wednesday; March, November and December, weekends only. Tel: 01295 760205.

The Washington family arms above the front door may have inspired the design of the American flag

During the restoration of the Great Hall a silver sixpence dated 1568, an Elizabethan baby's shoe and a decorated knife case (thought to have belonged to Lawrence Washington) were discovered in a crevice between the ceiling and the floor above.

Queen Victoria stayed at
Wimpole in 1843 and this
event is now commemorated
annually by school children
donning the costumes of
servants and preparing for
the royal visit.

WIMPOLE HALL
Cambridgeshire

6 MILES (9.5 KM) NORTH OF ROYSTON

*T*he largest house in the county, Wimpole Hall is interesting on several counts. It was begun in the 17th century and continued to develop over the years – unremarkable in itself, for many houses followed this course, but it is the number of important architects who had a hand in that development which distinguishes Wimpole.

James Gibbs was responsible for the wonderfully elegant painted library built to house the famous Harley collection of 50,000 books, 40,000 prints and 300,000 pamphlets – all sold to meet financial demands made on the 2nd Earl of Oxford's widow. (Part of the collection was later purchased to form the basis of the British Library.) Henry Flitcroft was commissioned to create the gallery and saloon, and the drawing room is the work of Sir John Soane. Victorian additions by Kendall were later removed.

After a short time in the ownership of the Duke of Newcastle and his heir, the 2nd Earl of Oxford, in the early 18th century, the Hall was bought by the 1st Earl of Harwicke. The 5th Earl was the last member of that family to occupy Wimpole Hall and in 1938 it was bought by Captain George Bambridge and his wife Elsie, one of Rudyard Kipling's daughters. By this time it was almost derelict and most of the contents of the house had been sold.

It was the Bambridges who decided to demolish most of Kendall's Victorian additions, making the house more faithful to its original design. They then set about the mammoth task of restoring and furnishing the Hall, and it was their loving care and tireless hard work that made Wimpole what it is today. On Mrs Bambridge's death in 1976 the property was bequeathed to the National Trust.

The splendid proportions of Wimpole Hall, below and right, owe their origin to a number of famous architects through the ages

One of the most stunning rooms is Sir John Soane's Yellow Drawing Room, but it is in very close competition with the magnificently decorated baroque chapel in the east wing, with its *trompe-l'oeil* ceiling, this time the creation of Sir James Thornhill. In contrast to all this finery, a glimpse of 'life below stairs' can be seen in the dry store, butler's pantry and the housekeeper's room in the basement.

If the Hall is remarkable for the number of great architects employed there, then the surrounding parkland can make a similar claim. It was transformed by no less than four of the country's most renowned landscape designers – Charles Bridgeman, 'Capability' Brown, Sanderson Miller and Humphrey Repton. The historic Home Farm, designed by Sir John Soane and including a range of buildings and rare breeds of farm animals, is also open to the public.

Open from mid-March to October on most days. Tel: 01223 207257.

This lovely hall, above and right, is still the home of the Rowley-Conwys

BODRHYDDAN
Clwyd

1½ MILES (2.5 KM) EAST OF RHUDDLAN

Bodrhyddan Hall is the home of Lord Langford, whose family name of Rowley-Conwy has appeared in local annals since the 13th century. The Hall dates back to the 15th century and there are many Tudor features still in evidence, but much of its present appearance dates from the 1870s when it was enlarged and remodelled by the architect Robert Nesfield at the request of Conwy Grenville Hercules Rowley-Conwy. One of the most radical changes was to construct a new main entrance facing west, giving the Hall a typical William and Mary façade. Since this time, very little alteration has been made.

The Rowley-Conwys have amassed a fascinating collection of unusual items over the centuries, including two mummy cases and smaller items brought back by Charlotte Rowley and her husband from their honeymoon in Egypt in 1836. Interestingly, one of the sons of the current owner spotted, completely by chance, the names of his great-great-grandparents carved into a column in the Mortuary Temple of Rameses III while visiting Thebes in 1978. The front hall has a collection of

arms and armour, most from around the time of the Civil War, but with two 15th-century *cap-à-pie* suits from Augsburg which may well have seen action at the Battle of Bosworth Field in 1485, and a collection of Oriental arms and armour. Naval and regimental swords used by the family are also on display here.

In the Great Hall are two portraits, unusual in that they are painted on wood, bearing the date 1606 and believed to be of William Conwy and his wife. Also here is an ornamental wooden chest, thought to have been a gift to the family from Charles II. The 'big' dining room was added to the house at the end of the 18th century and though rarely used these days for its original purpose, provides a lovely showcase for the collection of family portraits. The largest picture in the room is that of Frances, Lady Stapleton, painted in 1701.

Until 1951, the White Drawing Room was the library – a dark and forbidding room, with its carvings painted in a dismal dark brown. Lord Langford remodelled and redecorated the room in white and gold, disposed of any books which were not of Welsh, local or family interest and installed the attractive collection of china which is now displayed here.

Open from June to September on selected afternoons, by appointment. Tel: 01745 590357.

BRYN BRAS CASTLE
Gwynedd

4 MILES (6.5 KM) EAST OF CAERNARFON

Visitors to Bryn Bras Castle may be forgiven for assuming that this is a medieval castle, adapted for comfortable family living. It was, in fact, not built until 1830, probably by architect Thomas Hopper though this is not known for certain. The castle enjoys a wonderful setting amidst beautiful gardens, with a backdrop of the high mountain scenery of Snowdonia.

The history of the castle's ownership is a chequered one. It was built for an attorney at law, Thomas Williams and his wife Lauretta Panton, but after his death in 1874 the property changed hands a number of times. At one point, before it was acquired by its present owners in 1965, it was owned by millionaire Duncan Elliot Alves. In spite of its somewhat remote location the castle has witnessed many lively social gatherings, with Edward, Prince of Wales and Lloyd George among its house-guests.

The building itself changed and developed over the years too; major alterations were made in the 1920s, including the installation of the striking stained-glass windows. There is a magnificent galleried staircase, and in the library are some unusual wood carvings and a painting by Bernard Gribble of Henry VIII leaving for the Field of the Cloth of Gold.

Open from Spring Bank Holiday to September daily, except Saturday. Tel: 01286 870210.

The drawing room, decorated in a cool green

ERDDIG
Clwyd

2 MILES (3 KM) SOUTH OF WREXHAM

No-one, least of all the National Trust, who now have the care of Erddig, would claim that the house is an architectural masterpiece, but its importance today and its source of fascination to visitors lies in the vivid insight it provides into the social and working life of a great country house.

In recognition of this, the tour of the house and estate begins at the working end of the scale, where the carpenters, blacksmiths, stable-hands and laundry-maids toiled away their working lives. The workshops are fully equipped and the sawmill building has a display of photographs and a video showing the restoration work carried out at Erddig.

After passing through the kitchens and servants' hall, visitors reach the grand neo-classical rooms that were occupied by the Yorke family until the 1970s. They are still furnished with the wonderful collection of gilt and silver furniture amassed by John Mellor, ancestor of the Yorkes, who bought Erddig from its original owner in 1716. Perhaps the most remarkable piece of furniture is the shining gold and cream state bed, with Chinese silk hangings. In contrast are the attic bedrooms where the maids slept and the nearby workroom where they spent their sparse moments of leisure.

Open from April to September daily, except Thursday and Friday. Tel: 01978 355314.

The magnificent state bed was very nearly lost at a time when the house was in a bad state of repair, and rain poured through the collapsing plaster ceiling of the bedroom through the tester and into buckets placed on the bed! However, after two years in the conservation department of the Victoria and Albert Museum this wonderful piece of furniture has been restored to its original condition.

The house is popular for the insight it gives into the smooth running of a country house

LLANCAIACH FAWR MANOR
Mid Glamorgan

TREHARRIS, 7 MILES (11.5 KM) SOUTH OF MERTHYR TYDFIL

A wonderfully entertaining tour of this fine old Tudor manor house re-creates life here during the Civil War, not simply through the accurate restoration of the house and furniture, but also by means of actor-guides. Dressed in the costume of the day, and speaking in the dialect of the 17th century, they take visitors around the house and recount historical facts and anecdotes to illustrate what life would have been like in those days. Visitors can enter into the spirit of things too, by putting on costumes – and even armour – and by trying their hand at some of the kitchen skills, such as making a clove pomander or crushing herbs.

The Manor was built by the Pritchard family in 1530, and as they prospered, so the house developed and expanded, with various alterations being made to it over the years.

During the Civil War, in August 1645, Charles I came to Llancaiach Fawr, an event which for some reason prompted Colonel Pritchard to switch his allegiance from the King to Parliament. Unfortunately, no record has been found to explain what precipitated this change of heart, though it may well have saved the Manor from the damage which befell so many homes of Royalists when Cromwell finally triumphed.

Open all year daily, except 25 and 26 December and 1 January. Tel: 01443 412248.

A mysterious switching of allegance is one of the stories associated with this old house

An extraordinary and delightful Victorian folly

PENRHYN CASTLE
Gwynedd

3 MILES (5 KM) EAST OF BANGOR

Building a vast Victorian mansion in the style of a Norman castle is not unheard of, but what makes Penrhyn Castle so unusual is that, whereas most such structures are simply a façade concealing a comfortable range of family rooms, here the theme continues throughout the interior. The grand staircase is quite startling in both its proportions – three full storeys high – and its cathedral-like structure of lofty arches, carved stone-work and stained glass.

Thomas Hopper was the architect who created this imaginatively forbidding structure for George Dawkins-Pennant, conveniently a local quarry owner, in 1820, and his commission also included the suitable fitting out of the interiors with panelling, plasterwork and furniture. Most of the furniture is also 19th-century 'Norman', and includes a slate bed weighing over a ton, and a brass bed made specially for Edward VII at the then huge cost of £600. The most notable of the rooms includes the Great Hall, which is heated by the Roman hypocaust method of under-floor hot air, the wonderful library with its heavily decorated ceiling, and the dining room, covered with neo-Norman decoration.

There is an Industrial Railway Museum in the courtyard and 40 acres (16ha) of beautiful grounds overlooking the North Wales coast.

Open from April to October daily, except Tuesday. Tel: 01248 353084.

PLAS NEWYDD
Gwynedd

1 MILE (1.5 KM) SOUTH-WEST OF LLANFAIR P G

*I*t would be hard to find a more delightful location for a grand house such as this than on the sheltered east side of Anglesey with views across the Menai Straits to the mountains of Snowdonia. There has been a house on the site since the 16th century, but any evidence of it was swept away in the early 1800s by James Wyatt when he largely rebuilt it with both Gothic and neo-classical features.

Plas Newydd was the home of the Marquesses of Anglesey until 1976, when it was passed to the care of the National Trust, and there are reminders of the family, including the 1st Marquess, who commanded Wellington's cavalry at Waterloo and lost a leg in the last moments of the battle, all around the house. A collection of uniforms and head-dresses continues the military theme.

In the 1930s the 6th Marquess commissioned Rex Whistler to paint a huge mural in the dining room. The artist's largest work ever, it was completed just before World War II, during which he lost his life. The mural, featuring Whistler himself as a gardener, now forms the centrepiece of an exhibition of his work.

Open from April to September daily, except Saturday; in October, Friday and Sunday only. Tel: 01248 714795.

Plas Newydd is beautifully set on the Anglesey coast

PLAS-YN-RHIW
Gwynedd

4½ MILES (7 KM) NORTH-EAST OF ABERDARON

The house appears tucked firmly into its attractive garden

Hells Mouth Bay (Porth Neigwl in Welsh), named for its reputation as a graveyard for sailing ships, is hardly an inviting address and yet this small and delightful manor house is to be found on the west shore of the bay.

Dating back to the medieval period and predominantly Tudor, Plas-yn-Rhiw was extended in the 1630s and again in the 18th and 19th centuries. Later the house fell into a sad state of disrepair and stood empty and near-derelict for some years, but thankfully this little gem was rescued and restored by the National Trust.

The 50 acres (20ha) of gardens and grounds stretching right down to the shoreline were also reclaimed and replanted with rhododendrons, azaleas and some sub-tropical shrubs. Box hedges and grass paths divide the gardens and a stream and waterfall tumble down towards the bay, while behind the house is a snowdrop wood.

The house and grounds are at the centre of an estate which extends for a further 416 acres (168ha) and includes traditional Welsh cottages, an old windmill and the area known as Mynydd-y-Craig, a remote and dramatic stretch of Lleyn Peninsula coastline, also in the care of the Trust.

Open from April to October daily, except Saturday; in October, Sunday only. Tel: 01758 88219.

PLAS NEWYDD
Clwyd

LLANGOLLEN, 9 MILES (15 KM) SOUTH-WEST OF WREXHAM

The distinctive black and white façade, below, was added to the house after the death of its most famous occupants, but other traces of the Ladies of Llangollen remain, such as this carved doorway, right

Llangollen is best known today for its International Music Festival and for white-water canoeing on the river, but in the late 18th and early 19th centuries the town was more famous for the 'Two Ladies of Llangollen', and Plas Newydd was their home.

In 1776 two Irish aristocrats, Lady Eleanor Butler and her friend the Honourable Sarah Ponsonby, left Ireland with their maid Mary after considerable opposition from their families and set up house together at Plas Newydd.'

Their rejection of the traditional path taken by young ladies into marriage and fashionable society brought them a degree of notoriety to which their penchant for a somewhat mannish style of dressing only added. But it was their reputation for hospitality and sharp wit that attracted visitors to the house and earned them the friendship

and respect of the townsfolk of Llangollen. A steady stream of visitors made their way to Plas Newydd, among them the Duke of Wellington, the Duke of Gloucester, Sir Walter Scott, Wordsworth and Southey. Lord Byron sent them a complimentary copy of *The Corsair*, and many poems were written about them. Eccentricity was a popular trait, but these were extremely well-read and entertaining ladies who also took a delight in recounting gossip and scandal. They would often entertain countless visitors in a single day.

Though now a large and impressive black-and-white house, the original building was just a cottage. The two ladies transformed it, adding Gothic touches and indulging in their passion for heavily carved wood by accepting pieces from return visitors as 'a kind of passport'. The porch is particularly impressive, held aloft by two beautifully turned bed posts, and the stained glass in their new oriel windows was largely the gift of friends.

Eleanor and Sarah lived at Plas Newydd for over 50 years, Sarah being the last to die in 1831, after which it was taken over by two more ladies – Amelia Lolly and Charlotte Andrew who had been dubbed by the previous occupants as 'The Lollies and Trollies'. After their deaths, the house was acquired by a General Yorke who made substantial alterations, of which the striking black-and-white façade was one. The General did, however, share the ladies' passion for oak and much of the interior today is resplendent with examples of the wood-carver's art, including Sarah and Eleanor's pew from Llangollen church, now built into a window recess.

Open from April to October daily, otherwise by arrangement. Tel: 01978 861514.

One of the finest old fortified manor houses in Britain, Stokesay has remained remarkably intact over the years

STOKESAY CASTLE
Shropshire

1 MILE (1.5 KM) SOUTH OF CRAVEN ARMS

*E*asily visible to motorists heading down the A49, Stokesay Castle presents a picturesque and romantic ensemble of buildings distinguished by the projecting half-timbering surmounting the five-sided north tower. The building was begun in about 1240 by a member of the Say family and bought by Lawrence of Ludlow, a wealthy wool trader, some 40 years later. The building work continued until 1305. Lawrence's descendants lived in the house for nearly 300 years, then after a succession of owners it was given to English Heritage.

The castle is one of the best-preserved early fortified manor houses in England and has remained virtually unaltered since its medieval heyday.

For this we have to thank the fact that, though it was fortified, implying unsettled times, it had a remarkably uneventful history and even during the Civil War it was the adjacent church that was damaged.

The heart of the house was the magnificent Great Hall, a vast chamber where 700 years ago the family, their guests and their servants would congregate under the high timbered roof. The principal family room was the solar, still reached by an outside wooden staircase which has survived from the 13th century; its walls are covered with Jacobean panelling.

Open all year; between October and March, closed Monday and Tuesday. Tel: 01588 672544.

TREDEGAR HOUSE
Gwent

2 MILES (3 KM) WEST OF NEWPORT

*I*t is hard to believe that one of the most magnificent 17th-century mansions in Britain should have remained relatively unknown for so long. For 500 years it was the home of the great and powerful Morgan family, later Lords Tredegar, and has recently been splendidly restored by its current owners, Newport Borough Council. William Morgan was the man responsible for the original building which was financed by his advantageous marriage to his cousin Blanche Morgan, who owned great estates in Breconshire.

The most sumptuous room of all is the aptly named Gilt Room, always the showcase of the whole house, used for formal occasions and intended not merely to impress, but to overwhelm.

The pine panelled walls have been grained to give the appearance of walnut, and upon them hang such paintings as *The Glorification of Pope Urban VIII* by Pietro da Cortona. The state dining room, with its carved busts of Roman emperors, is almost as impressive.

But it is not just the high life which is portrayed at Tredegar. Below stairs, the butler's pantry, the plate scullery and the kitchen, complete with its elaborate spit mechanism, offer an insight into the working lives of the 22 indoor servants who once ensured the smooth running of the household.

Open Easter to September on most days and Wednesdays in October. Tel: 01633 815880.

Set in extensive grounds, Tredegar ranks among the best 17th century houses

WEOBLEY CASTLE
West Glamorgan

LLANRHIDIAN, 9 MILES (14.5 KM) WEST OF SWANSEA

*S*itting high above the north shore of the Gower peninsula, this impressive medieval fortified manor house was probably one of the earliest Norman settlements in this part of the country. Though its early history is rather sketchy, it is believed that by the 13th century Weobley belonged to the de la Bere family who were known to have had considerable holdings of land hereabouts and were most certainly well established by the 14th century. After peaceful beginnings, the early 15th century saw widespread disruption to the Gower (as to the whole of Wales) caused by the revolution led by Owain Glydwr, and it is likely that the castle was substantially damaged during the hostilities.

Prosperity returned to Weobley at the end of the 15th century when it came into the ownership of Sir Rhys ap Thomas, the most powerful Welshman of that era – principally because of his

The old house at Weobley has had a chequered history

support for Henry VII at the Battle of Bosworth in 1485 which led to the Welsh Tudor dynasty taking the throne of England. Weobley was substantially rebuilt in order to transform it into a home befitting such a prominent man, but the family fell foul of the monarchy when Sir Rhys' grandson, Rhys ap Gruffudd was executed for treason.

Weobley then became the property of the King but was later sold to Sir William Herbert, Earl of Pembroke – another important and influential figure. The Herberts kept the castle for the next 100 years or so, but it was no longer an important residence – it had again fallen into disrepair and was leased out as a farmhouse. Between 1666 and 1911 Weobley Castle was in the ownership of the Mansel and the Talbot families; it is now in the care of CADW, the organisation which cares for historic monuments in Wales.

There are substantial remains of the castle to be seen today, with buildings grouped around a courtyard. The south-west tower is probably the oldest part, though all of the main structure was in place by the early 14th century. It is important to imagine the rooms here as they would have been then, as comfortable family apartments with the stonework covered with plaster and hung with tapestries, and logs burning in the capacious fireplaces.

The solar, which would once have been the lord's private chamber, now houses an exhibition relating the story of Weobley Castle.

Open all year daily, except Christmas and New Year. Tel: 01792 390012.

Fire damage in 1861 resulted in substantial rebuilding of parts of the house by the great Victorian architect Anthony Salvin

CAPESTHORNE HALL
Cheshire

5 MILES (8 KM) WEST OF MACCLESFIELD

The industrious Dame Dorothy Davenport (1562–1639) spent 26 years completing the needlework for the great four-poster bed in the room now named after her

The Bromley-Davenports can trace their ancestry back to the Norman Conquest, and their ownership of the Capesthorne estate was recorded in the Domesday Book. The present house, dating from the early 18th century with substantial Victorian alterations, replaced a timber-framed building on the site. Although even its owners are reluctant to call it beautiful, with its blackened towers and pinnacles above the red-brick façades it has immense character; it is also packed with all kinds of treasures.

Much of the charm of Capesthorne lies in its variety. There are sumptuous state rooms – the dining room is particularly striking – which contrast with such rooms as the delightful American Room, furnished in colonial style from the Philadelphia home of the present Lady Bromley-Davenport. There is the Dorothy Davenport Room, with its splendid Jacobean four-poster bed, and the state bedroom, containing the chairs used by the family at the coronation of Queen Elizabeth II. The material on the bedhead is the same as that used at Westminster Abbey. Fine classical marbles and busts adorn the sculpture gallery, and beneath it all the cellars have various displays and exhibitions, including an array of Civil War armour.

Surrounding the hall are beautiful gardens and grounds, with lakes and woodland.

Open April to September on selected days. Tel: 01625 861221 or 861779.

CASTLE HOWARD
North Yorkshire

5½ MILES (9 KM) SOUTH-WEST OF MALTON

Magnificent in its design and palatial in its proportions, Castle Howard is one of our greatest 'stately homes'. Built for the powerful 3rd Earl of Carlisle, Charles Howard (and still occupied by his descendants), it was begun in 1699 and was the first architectural commission of Sir John Vanbrugh, also a successful playwright whose theatricality is evident amidst all the grandeur here. He incorporated into its design the first dome ever to be built on a private house in England; in fact, unhindered as he was by formal training, Vanbrugh employed many innovative devices in this building.

The Great Hall is cathedral-like, stretching 70ft (21m) from ground level right up into the dome, with enormous columns and elaborate decoration. A series of breathtaking rooms stretching out from this central glory await the visitor – richly coloured and sumptuously decorated state rooms filled with superb furniture and works of art, including paintings by Holbein, Gainsborough, Reynolds and Rubens.

The Museum Room displays the works of the 9th Earl of Carlisle, a noted artist, and of his friends, while the long south gallery has family and royal portraits. The beautiful chapel, still used for services, has wonderful stained glass designed by Burne-Jones.

Open from mid-March to October daily. Tel: 01653 648333.

The great central dome was the first to be built on a private house

CRAGSIDE
Northumberland

2 MILES (3 KM) NORTH OF ROTHBURY

Cragside was built as the weekend retreat for the 1st Lord Armstrong, who had two successful careers, first as a lawyer, then as an inventor, engineer and gunmaker. He founded the company which was to become Vickers Armstrong in later years.

Cragside began modestly, but gradually expanded into a proper country mansion with a wildly picturesque outline, well suited to the rugged wooded hills which surround it. Not surprisingly, Armstrong's scientific bent was put to use here – Cragside was the earliest house in the world to be lit by hydro-electricity, and the kitchen has a hydraulic service lift and a spit powered from a lake above the house. The family used to say he 'had water on the brain'!

The many rooms within the house vary considerably in size and character. The drawing room is very grand with a double-storey chimney-piece of Italian marble, and the dining room, in Old English style, is one of the finest Victorian domestic rooms in the country. The library, with its light oak panelling and elaborate ceiling, is one of the most attractive rooms, and the study is cosy and inviting.

In contrast to all this 'Englishness' is the Japanese Room, named after the 19th-century prints on its walls, and the Bamboo Room, filled with simulated bamboo furniture.

Open from April to October daily except Monday, but open on Bank Holidays. Tel: 01669 20333.

The drawing room is dominated by the extraordinary carved fireplace

GAWSWORTH HALL
Cheshire

GAWSWORTH, 2½ MILES (4 KM) SOUTH OF MACCLESFIELD

Gawsworth Hall was once the home of England's last professional jester

A fine example of Cheshire black-and-white architecture, Gawsworth Hall was built in the second half of the 15th century and for many years was the home of the Fitton family. Today it is a peaceful and serene household, giving little hint of its eventful past.

They were known as the 'Fighting Fittons' in those days, and Mary Fitton, 'the wayward maid of Gawsworth', is said to be the 'Dark Lady' of Shakespeare's sonnets. The last professional jester in England, Maggoty Johnson, lived at Gawsworth where he was dancing master to the children, and is buried nearby in 'Maggoty Johnson's Wood'.

Originally the house was built around a quadrangle, but it was reduced in size by Charles Gerard, 2nd Earl of Macclesfield, around the end of the 17th century. Today it has all the charm and character of a medieval house, with fine old timbers and ornate fireplaces, and is filled with comfortable old furniture, paintings, sculpture and armour. The delightful little chapel has beautiful stained glass by Burne-Jones and William Morris, while out in the lovely grounds is a rare survivor – an Elizabethan tilting ground.

Open mid-March to early October, every afternoon. Tel: 01260 223456.

HAREWOOD HOUSE
West Yorkshire

HAREWOOD, 6 MILES (9.5 KM) SOUTH OF HARROGATE

*T*he home of the Lascelles family for over 200 years, Harewood House is an exquisite example of the work of both John Carr of York, the original architect, and Robert Adam who was brought in at a later date to design all the interiors. Even the furniture was specially made for the house by Thomas Chippendale, who was born at nearby Otley in the Wharfe Valley. But even though it is hailed as a showpiece of 18th-century architecture, things haven't stood still at Harewood and alterations were made in Victorian times by Sir Charles Barry, architect of the Houses of Parliament. He added a third storey and transformed the south façade with an Italianate terrace.

An ancient family, one of whom came to Britain with William the Conqueror, the Lascelles increased their fortune through their Barbados sugar plantations in the late 17th century, facilitating the building of their new mansion at Harewood. Subsequent generations added the fine art collections – the first Viscount Lascelles amassed the collection of Chinese celadon and French porcelain

Below and right, Harewood House is a splendid example of 18th-century architecture

and commissioned watercolours from the leading artists of the day. The 6th Earl of Harewood, the present earl's father, put together a splendid collection of Italian paintings, and with his wife, Princess Mary, the Princess Royal, set about the restoration of the house, bringing back some of the character which Robert Adam had intended it should have.

The house has been open to visitors almost since it was built, when interested sightseers were taken round by arrangement with the housekeeper. Today, most of the original building is on show and the family's private apartments are on the top floor. The entrance hall, with its fine plasterwork and classical lines, shows Robert Adam's unity of style to perfection but today it is dominated by the most important modern work of art in the house – Jacob Epstein's statue of Adam (the biblical one). From here a tour of the house takes in magnificent formal state rooms and such wonderfully welcoming and comfortable rooms as Lord Harewood's sitting room and the lovely old library.

In every one of the rooms is a stunning array of works of art, fine china and beautiful furniture, mingled with family photographs and memorabilia. In addition to the fine paintings in the house, the terrace gallery stages a programme of temporary exhibitions, and beyond the terrace are lovely grounds, with a lake and a famous bird garden.

Open from mid-March to October, daily. Tel: 01532 886225.

Attractive gardens surround this family home

HOLKER HALL
Cumbria

3 MILES (5 KM) WEST OF GRANGE-OVER-SANDS

Henry Cavendish, grandson of the 2nd Duke of Devonshire, was a scientist – he discovered nitric acid and the properties of hydrogen, and also calculated the density of the Earth. Henry was a recluse, but his heir was allowed to visit him for half an hour every year.

*O*ne of the nice things about Holker Hall is that visitors are encouraged to wander at will and take their time over every room, without the constraints of ropes, barriers or tour guides. And it is very much a lived-in home, with all the warmth and character that families bring to what could otherwise be just a museum piece.

The first impression of Holker is of a grand Victorian mansion, but its heart is the 16th-century home of the Prestons, from whom it has passed by marriage and inheritance to the Cavendish family, now living there. Cavendish is the family name of the Dukes of Devonshire, and the Holker Cavendishes are a branch of that family.

Their home, rebuilt in grand Victorian style after a fire in 1871, is utterly charming, combining superb plasterwork, panelling and works of art with delightful country-house furnishings in some of the rooms. The Duke's bedroom, with its deep-red walls and oak panelling, is particularly striking. The Long Gallery is a recreation of Elizabethan-style galleries, the dining room has a wonderful carved oak fireplace, and the drawing room retains its original silk wall coverings.

Various exhibitions at Holker include a collection of antique kitchen appliances, a photographic exhibition and a motor museum, and there are award-winning gardens.

Open from April to October daily, except Saturday. Tel: 01539 558328.

LEVENS HALL
Cumbria

5 MILES (8 KM) SOUTH OF KENDAL

ontinuity is associated with Levens Hall, for not only has it been in the family for around 700 years, but many of the members of staff that visitors encounter have followed in the footsteps of their forebears. The overall impression is that Levens Hall is cared for by all who are involved with it.

Dating from around the middle of the 13th century, the house was considerably altered and enlarged in the 16th, and again around the turn of the 17th and 18th centuries.

Apart from the intricate plaster ceilings, the Hall is distinguished particularly by the wonderful oak panelling in most of the rooms, much of it made in Warwick and transported to Levens by canal. All around the house the family history comes to life. The drawing room has showcases with documents and domestic paperwork, and the Redman Dressing Room has the earliest English patchwork (1703), painstakingly worked from tiny pieces of Indian cotton with 32 stitches to the inch. The musem includes the page's costume worn by Charles Bagot at the coronation of George IV. There is also a fine collection of clocks, following the interest of the current owner, Charles Henry (Hal) Bagot. Outside is the famous and historic topiary garden.

Open from April to September daily, except Friday and Saturday. Tel: 01539 560321.

The Bagot family have the distinction of sharing their name with a rare breed of goat, specimens of which roam in the Levens parkland.

A thick, castellated hedge separates the Hall from the garden to the south

LITTLE MORETON HALL
Cheshire

4 MILES (6.5 KM) SOUTH-WEST OF CONGLETON

ittle Moreton Hall is one of the most famous and best-preserved timbered houses in the country. Built within a moat and around a delightful cobbled courtyard, its exterior is a riot of black-and-white patterns, each square panel containing a rich variety of designs. The windows, too, are intricately glazed, again with various patterns picked out by the strips of lead. The Hall was begun in the middle of the 15th century for the Moreton family, powerful local landlords and tax collectors for the king,

Below and right, the crazy angles and black-and-white patterning give Little Moreton Hall a wonderful air of eccentricity

and further extensions were added up to 1580. The family continued to live there, except for a break of about 200 years when it was let out to tenants, until it was finally donated to the National Trust in 1937.

The east wing and the Great Hall, once the focus of day-to-day life on the estate, are the oldest parts of the house. Three items of furniture here are original to the house – the long refectory table, the 'great rounde table' which occupies the bay window and the 'cubborde of boxes'. Apart from

The original garderobes (lavatories) at Little Moreton Hall are preserved intact. In those days the effluent would have been collected and spread on the surrounding fields – there was no alternative to organic farming.

these items, the rooms in the Hall are largely empty. No doubt authentic pieces with which to refurnish the house are not easy to come by, and the lack of them only serves to emphasise the wonderful architecture and proportions of each room.

The withdrawing room was the place to which the lord of the manor, his family and guests could retreat from the noise of the Great Hall and enjoy some privacy from the servants. Here the enormous roof timbers are moulded, and there is a magnificent overmantel carved with the royal arms of Elizabeth I.

When the house was extended in the 16th century the chapel was built, although the stained glass was not added until 1932. The panels of text are taken from the 1539 edition of the Tyndale Bible.

The upper storey of the south wing of the house is occupied by the superb Long Gallery, which stretches for 68ft (20m) beneath massive arch-braced roof trusses. The gallery would always have been relatively free of furniture for its main purpose was for daily exercise and games – and a 17th-century tennis ball was found behind one of the panels.

Within the moated area of the house there is a formal knot garden, a charming replica of a typical 17th-century design.

Open from late March to October on selected afternoons. Tel: 01260 272018.

*Mirehouse proudly proclaims
its literary connections*

✽
MIREHOUSE
Cumbria

3 MILES (5 KM) NORTH OF KESWICK
✽
---

*'Mirehouse was beautiful and
so were the ways of it...not to
speak of Skiddaw and the
finest mountains of the earth.'*
Thomas Carlyle

The Lake District is famed for its literary associations and Mirehouse can claim its share of these. In the 19th century it came into the ownership of John Spedding, who went to school with Wordsworth and maintained a life-long friendship with the poet. John's sons, Thomas and James, were of a more literary persuasion than their father and collected a circle of close friends who included the Scottish historian and writer Thomas Carlyle, Edward FitzGerald, who translated *The Rubaiyat of Omar Khayyam*, Thackeray, and Alfred Lord Tennyson, who worked on his *Morte D'Arthur* and many other works at Mirehouse. James Spedding devoted his life to the study of Francis Bacon, writing his biography in no less than 14 volumes.

Mirehouse, standing in the shadow of the Skiddaw range of mountains, has a series of richly decorated and comfortably furnished rooms which speak eloquently of the Spedding's literary connections. The smoking room contains James's collection of first editions of Bacon's work and his research papers into Bacon's life. The drawing room is dominated by a splendid portrait of James, and there are others of Tennyson, Arthur Hallam and other writers of the day, including a drawing of Tennyson by James Spedding himself. A painting of Antony Spedding's Hampstead home by John Constable, another family friend, also hangs here.

Open from April to October on selected afternoons. Tel: 017687 72287.

NEWBY HALL
North Yorkshire

4 MILES (6.5 KM) SOUTH-EAST OF RIPON

The early history of Newby Hall is something of a mystery, although a property was recorded here in the 13th century. The present house dates from the late 17th century and was built for William Weddell, who had returned from his Grand Tour of Europe with such a large collection of works of art that he needed a suitably grand home in which to display them to proper effect. Among his purchases were superb classical sculptures and a set of Gobelin tapestries.

When it came to designing a suitable setting for Weddell's treasures, one name sprang immediately to mind and that was Robert Adam, the foremost classical architect of his age. The entrance hall, library and sculpture gallery show his work at its very best, and the wonderful Tapestry Room, surviving in its entirety, demonstrates Adam's skill at creating unity between the décor and contents of a room.

Other rooms have developed over the years to suit the needs of the succession of owners and are a delightful mixture of styles and colour schemes, but the recently decorated drawing room has gone back to Adam's original scheme. The dining room is an elegant Regency addition to the Hall, and the lovely gardens which surround the house were largely created by the present owner's father.

Open from April to September every afternoon except Monday, but open on Bank Holidays. Tel: 01423 322583.

In the 17th century the gardener was the most highly paid of the Newby Hall staff, earning £16 a year. The cook was second at £10 and the brewer earned £8, twice as much as the butler, who was then some way down the hierarchy of domestic staff. The poor poultry maid had to manage on £1. 15s.

'This is the finest house I saw in Yorkshire.'
Celia Fiennes, on her tour of the north in 1697

This lovely house is set in a beautiful garden, with borders sweeping down to the river

*Portraits and hunting scenes
adorn the walls of the hall*

NORTON CONYERS
North Yorkshire

3½ MILES (5.5 KM) NORTH-WEST OF RIPON

Devotees of Charlotte Brontë's *Jane Eyre*, visiting Norton Conyers, will find that it matches quite remarkably the description of Thornfield Hall in the book. Charlotte Brontë visited the house about eight years before her novel was published and while she was there heard the family story of a mad woman who was kept in the attic – her model for Mrs Rochester, perhaps.

The history of the Grahams of Norton Conyers is one of ups and downs. A wild and unruly bunch, they came from Scotland in the early 17th century. However, one younger son went to London in the service of the Duke of Buckingham, rose to be one of Charles I's Gentlemen of the Horse and came back a baronet. Loyalty to the crown cost them dearly after the Civil War, but the Restoration brought new honour and several royal visits to their home. The 4th Baronet was poisoned, albeit accidentally, and the 7th squandered away the family fortune and most of its property, including Norton Conyers. Fortunately his son married an heiress and was able to buy it back.

The house has seen many changes since it was first built in the mid-14th century, with substantial alterations being carried out towards the end of the 18th century. There are fine portraits all around the house and some excellent pieces of furniture, including the long table in the hall which dates from the Middle Ages. The library contains a collection of costumes dating from the 1880s, and further costumes and family wedding dresses are on show in the 'best' spare room. King James's Room, where James II stayed when he was Duke of York, is furnished in 17th-century style.

Open late May to early September on selected days. Tel: 01765 640333.

RYDAL MOUNT
Cumbria

1½ MILES (2.5 KM) NORTH OF AMBLESIDE

*I*n 1813 William Wordsworth brought his family to Rydal Mount and he stayed here until his death in 1850, drawing inspiration from the wonderful lakeland views from the house. The family he brought with him included not only his wife and daughter, but his sister Dorothy. However, family life was not all happiness and contentment. Dorothy's protracted descent into mental illness caused him great sorrow, and when his beloved daughter, Dora, died, he was inconsolable. There were, of course, many happy times too, and Wordsworth frequently played host to other literary figures, including Coleridge and Matthew Arnold.

The house is now owned by a descendant of the poet, and the living rooms and bedrooms which the Wordsworths occupied are on show to visitors, along with the study he built onto the house. The room above the stables, used as a schoolroom for Dora Wordsworth, has a special display and a shop selling books and souvenirs.

All around the house are family portraits, personal possessions and first editions of Wordsworth's work, but his presence is felt most, perhaps, in the lovely gardens which he designed and created himself, and where he would pace up and down, formulating his verse.

Open from February to November on most days. Tel: 01539 433002.

Rydal Mount is in a magnificent setting, a garden lovingly created by Wordsworth

An ancient pele tower stands at the heart of the old house

SIZERGH CASTLE
Cumbria

3½ MILES (5.5 KM) SOUTH OF KENDAL

Sir Thomas Strickland had the honour of carrying the banner of St George – England's premier banner – to the Battle of Agincourt in 1415.

There is a great 14th-century tower at the heart of Sizergh Castle, the original part of a building which had the misfortune to be within a wide band of the country which, at that time, frequently changed hands between England and Scotland. This pele tower is still recognisable, but a great deal of building was done during Tudor times, extending the castle to the north and west and adding a great chamber over the old hall.

Most of the interior now reflects this time of prosperity and expansion, with superb oak panelling and some outstanding carving. The intricately inlaid panelling of the Inlaid Chamber was sold in 1891 to the Victoria and Albert Museum, but they have kindly loaned two panels back to Sizergh so that visitors can imagine how the room would have looked. The museum also loaned the inlaid bed, which had been made to match the room.

In 1239 Sizergh Castle was brought into the Strickland family by its heiress, and their descendant still lives here today, although the family gave the castle to the National Trust in 1950. Their occupancy of the castle was unbroken throughout that period except for a short time when the family accompanied James II into exile. Their support of the Stuart cause is reflected in many of the portraits in the house.

Open from April to October every afternoon, except Friday and Saturday. Tel: 01539 560070.

SLEDMERE HOUSE
Humberside

7 MILES (11.5 KM) NORTH-WEST OF DRIFFIELD

When 'Capability' Brown was commissioned to landscape the grounds in the 1770s he demolished the old village and rebuilt it out of sight on the eastern boundary of the estate.

Thanks to careful restoration and sensitive extension after a fire in Edwardian times, Sledmere House is still essentially Georgian in appearance. It was originally built by Sir Christopher Sykes, 2nd Baronet, in the 1750s and is particularly notable for its wonderful decorative plasterwork. This was carried out by the leading exponent of the craft, Joseph Rose, and luckily some of his work escaped the destruction of the fire. The painted and gilded ceiling of the drawing room is a particularly fine example.

The rooms here are furnished and decorated in keeping with the period of the house and there are some particularly attractive four-poster beds. The fine works of art include several portraits by Sir Peter Lely. There is the unexpected, too, in the form of the ornate Turkish Room, a copy of one of the Sultan's apartments in the Valideh Mosque in Istanbul. It serves as a memorial to the 6th Baronet, Sir Mark Sykes, an eminent orientalist and government negotiator in eastern affairs.

Sledmere's library is in the style of a classical Long Gallery, a suitable setting for the outstanding collection of books amassed by Sir Christopher and his son, but, sadly, sold off in 1824. Today the shelves are lined with an interesting rather than unique selection of reading matter.

Open at Easter, on selected afternoons in April and every afternoon from May to September. Tel: 01377 236637.

The lovely gilded drawing room

Part of the unusual painted hall

WALLINGTON HOUSE
Northumberland

CAMBO, 10 MILES (16 KM) WEST OF MORPETH

*A*t the heart of a great moorland estate, this great, square William and Mary mansion has a surprise for visitors. In the midst of all its splendour and its exceptionally beautiful plasterwork, its exquisite collections of porcelain and its fine works of art, Wallington's central hall is a curiosity. It is a grand, galleried hall made cosy; a lofty formal area altered to be lived in. The pillars and arches are painted with plants and flowers, undertaken by Lady Trevelyan and her friends (including John Ruskin), and the main panels are painted with dramatic scenes from Northumbrian history by William Bell Scott. Sir William and Lady Trevelyan were renowned for their eccentricity and charm, and this room is a fitting illustration of their occupancy of Wallington.

Elsewhere in the house visitors will be charmed again, by the collection of dolls' houses and model soldiers, by the kitchen, filled with Victorian utensils and appliances, and by Lady Wilson's Cabinet of Curiosities – a diverse collection which includes antiquities, stuffed birds, narwhal tusks, documents relating to Wallington and a model of a Jerusalem church. The house is set in 100 acres (40ha) of lawns, lakes and woodland, with a lovely walled garden and a conservatory housing tender plants.

Open from April to October every afternoon, except Tuesday. Tel: 01670 74283.

WASHINGTON OLD HALL
Tyne & Wear

WASHINGTON, 5 MILES (8 KM) WEST OF SUNDERLAND

Due to its name as much as anything, Washington Old Hall is most famous as the ancestral home of the Washington family whose descendant, George, became the first President of the United States of America. The link may be somewhat tenuous – the Washington family left the house in 1613, long before George's great-grandfather emigrated – but the connection is still acknowledged and there are celebrations are usually hel   here on the 4th of July for American Independence Day.

When the Washingtons left the Old Hall it was bought by the Bishop of Durham for his son, Francis James, who largely rebuilt the medieval house, but after that its history becomes obscure. It certainly declined in importance until, in the 19th century, it was occupied by as many as 11 of the poorest families in the area. In danger of demolition in the 1930s, Washington Old Hall was saved by a preservation committee and has since been carefully restored.

It was handed over to the National Trust in 1956 and is now furnished as for the gentry of the Jacobean period, with heavy, carved oak furniture, Delftware and a fine collection of paintings. There are exhibitions on George Washington and about the restoration of the property, and a Jacobean garden is being re-created.

Open from April to October daily, except Friday and Saturday. Tel: 0191-416 6879.

The American link may be uncertain, but this is still a fascinating house to visit

Abbotsford stands on the site of the last of the clan battles in the Borders, a fact which is wholly in keeping with Sir Walter Scott's romantic view of historical events and which may even have influenced his choice of a new home.

ABBOTSFORD
Borders

2 MILES (3 KM) WEST OF MELROSE

Sir Walter Scott's lovely mansion on the River Tweed is a reminder of a great man

*A*bbotsford is fascinating on two counts – first because it was the home of Sir Walter Scott, and second because of the diverse collections with which the writer filled his house. Many of these collections were brought with him from his former home, just a few miles away at Ashiestiel, and it is said to have been a curious procession which moved up the valley to Abbotsford on 28 May 1812. By this time Sir Walter was already a published writer, with the profits from *The Lay of the Last Minstrel*, *Marmion* and *The Lady of the Lake* contributing to the purchase of his new home. Two years after moving in he began his *Waverley* series of novels, and as his success as a writer grew, so too did Abbotsford and its estate.

In 1818 the former farmhouse was extended by the addition of an armoury, a dining room, a study, a conservatory and three extra bedrooms. Then in 1822 the original building was demolished to make way for what is now the main block of Abbotsford. By this time Sir Walter's holdings of land had increased to some 1,400 acres (567ha), which he liberally planted with trees. The house was further extended in the 1850s by Sir Walter's descendant, Walter Lockhart Scott, who added a west wing containing the chapel and kitchen, thus completing the attractive composition we see today.

Successive generations of Scotts have made Abbotsford their home, but it remains a splendid memorial to their famous ancestor and all around the house are reminders of him. The study is particularly evocative, with a bronze cast of his head still watching over his writing desk, and shelves and shelves of books which have spilled over from the library. Altogether there are about 9,000 volumes collected by Sir Walter. He looks out over the drawing room, too, from the famous portrait by Raeburn over the fireplace. This is a delightful room, with the Chinese hand-painted wallpaper given to Sir Walter by his cousin, and a roll-top desk and chairs given to him by George IV.

Sir Walter had a fascination for historic weaponry, and his armoury contains an interesting mixture ranging from his own blunderbuss to Rob Roy's broadsword, dirk and sporran purse. Bonnie Dundee's pistol is here, and the double-barrelled carbine of a Tyrolean patriot.

Other curiosities are dotted around the house, including various relics from the Battle of Waterloo, two cannon balls from the siege of Roxburgh Castle in 1460, a model of the skull of Robert the Bruce and a 'scold's bridle', used to silence nagging wives.

Open from late March to October daily. Tel: 01896 2043.

A Highland retreat fit for a queen

BALMORAL
Grampian

8 MILES (13 KM) WEST OF BALLATER

*I*n 1842 Queen Victoria and Prince Albert visited Scotland for the first time and were entranced both by the magnificence of the Highland scenery and the friendliness of the Scots. Subsequent visits reinforced their enthusiasm to such an extent that when the lease of a small Deeside castle and its estate became available they set negotiations in motion to secure Balmoral as their holiday home – without seeing it. However, when the couple arrived to take possession on 8 September 1848 they were not disappointed. The Queen described it as a 'pretty little castle in the old Scottish style' and the scenery as 'the finest almost I have seen anywhere'.

Victoria and Albert lived simply during their holidays at Balmoral, but the castle proved too small for their growing family and the procession of important visitors so, acquiring the freehold, they built a new castle in similar style 100yds (91m) from the original. That castle remains much the same today and is the favourite holiday home of the present royal family. Balmoral is also at the heart of a 50,000-acre (20,000ha) working estate of farms and forests.

In addition to the beautiful grounds, dotted with royal monuments, the ballroom of the castle houses an exhibition of paintings, porcelain and other items.

Open from May to July daily, except Sunday. Tel: 013397 42334/5.

HOUSE OF THE BINNS
Lothian

BLACKNESS, 4 MILES (6.5 KM) EAST OF LINLITHGOW

Two years of major structural restoration works have recently been completed at this fascinating house, predominantly a Regency mansion but also displaying the changing architectural tastes which have taken place here from 1612 onwards. It has evolved from a tall, grey, three-storeyed building with small windows and twin turrets into a pretty U-shaped house with crenellations and embellished windows. Inside, it has some beautiful early 17th-century moulded plaster ceilings.

Before coming into the care of the National Trust for Scotland, the House of The Binns had been the home of the Dalyell family since 1612. One of its most colourful characters was General Tam Dalyell, an ardent Royalist who was captured by Cromwell's army at the Battle of Worcester but escaped from the Tower of London and fled to Russia, where he organised the Tzar's army. He was recalled at the Restoration to command Charles II's forces in Scotland, and was the founder of the Royal Scots Greys in 1681. His boots and comb can still be seen in the house, together with a thimble belonging to his grand-daughter, Magdalen (who made a 'set of hingings for the whole hoose') and the drawings of Sir John Graham Dalyell, who taught Darwin.

Open June to September every afternoon, except Friday. Tel: 01506 834255.

A large pier-glass apparently doubles the size of this comfortable room

Culzean is superbly set on a cliff-top, with beautiful terraced gardens on the landward side

CULZEAN CASTLE
Strathclyde

4 MILES (6.5 KM) WEST OF MAYBOLE

W here once the medieval tower-house of the chiefs of the Clan Kennedy perched on its cliff-top, looking out towards Arran and Kintyre, there now stands one of 18th-century architect Robert Adam's finest works.

The great mansion was built during the 1770s for the 10th Earl of Cassillis, chief of the Kennedys, and remained in their family until it was given to the National Trust for Scotland in 1945. Since that time much restoration work has been carried out and the splendid state rooms once again show off the magnificent decorative plasterwork in the original colours specified in Adam's designs. The most notable features of the Culzean interiors are the oval staircase and the unusual circular drawing room with its specially woven carpet. The west wing of the castle dates from 1879, when the 14th Earl needed more space for his large family.

Culzean Castle also contains the National Guest Flat, an apartment which was given, after World War II, to US President Eisenhower for use during his lifetime. There is now an exhibition relating to Eisenhower's links with the castle.

As well as its beautiful gardens, the Culzean estate includes Scotland's first country park, established in 1969 and centred on the buildings of the former Home Farm.

Open from April to October daily. Tel: 016556 274.

HOUSE OF DUN
Tayside

4 MILES (6.5 KM) WEST OF MONTROSE

It would be difficult to select a highlight from a tour of the House of Dun, such is the quality and variety of its features and contents.

High on the list would be the building itself – a fine example of the work of William Adam dating from the 1730s – and another contender would be the wonderful plasterwork, which consists of a number of allegorical bas-reliefs, friezes and stucco work, most notable in the Saloon. There follows a series of less imposing, but utterly charming rooms, adorned with fine family portraits, china and clocks.

The bedrooms are also particularly interesting, with some beautiful embroidery, splendid tapestries and early examples of bathroom fittings, including a 19th-century boot bath (which actually looks like a boot) and an early, chain-operated shower bath.

Down in the basement, along with the former Servants' Hall are the Gun and Rod Rooms, complete with all the paraphernalia associated with the sports which once filled the larders. Here also is a delightful little model theatre – 'Mr Riach's Performing Theatre of Arts', which dates back to the 1830s. You can also tour the fully equipped and furnished kitchen, and the house-keeper's accommodation. Out in the courtyard, the Gamekeeper's Bothy and the Potting Shed provide an insight into some of the work of the estate.

Open at Easter, then from May to September daily; and weekends in October. Tel: 01674 810264.

The former carriage house of the House of Dun is now leased to the last handloom linen weaver working in Britain. Once a widespread occupation, linen weaving has now been taken over by machine-looms in factories, but here Ian Dale continues his craft and produces a fine range of traditional designs.

The fine old House of Dun is in the care of the National Trust for Scotland

Almost more like some Alpine château, Dunrobin stands high on an outcrop

DUNROBIN CASTLE
Highland

1 MILE (1.5 KM) NORTH-EAST OF GOLSPIE

Dunrobin is named after Earl Robin who built the original castle – a great square keep looking out over the sea from its cliff-top vantage point – here in the 13th century. The present Dunrobin Castle bears little resemblance, though, to that original tower, since it was rebuilt in the 19th century in the romantic Gothic style to a design by Sir Charles Barry (who also designed the Houses of Parliament).

With its gleaming towers and turrets, the seat of the Dukes of Sutherland certainly strikes a magnificent pose and is all the more interesting because older parts of the castle can still be distinguished amidst the Victorian building.

The interiors are no less impressive, with beautiful rooms furnished with fine French furniture, tapestries and paintings, including works by Canaletto. Many of the rooms, including the drawing room, dining room and library, reflect the involvement here of architect Sir Robert Lorimer in the early part of this century. He was a leading light in the Arts and Crafts movement, as the standard of workmanship ably demonstrates.

The castle is set in beautiful gardens which were laid out in grand style in the 19th century. The influence of Versailles on the garden design is unmistakable.

Open Easter, then mid-May to mid-October daily. Tel: 01408 633177 or 633268.

FALKLAND PALACE
Fife

FALKLAND, 4½ MILES (7 KM) NORTH-WEST OF GLEN ROTHES

The forbidding walls of Falkland Palace – likened by Thomas Carlyle to 'a black old bit of coffin or protrusive shin-bone sticking through the soil of the dead past' – encapsulate one of the most romantic periods of Scottish history. Here you will find tales of intrigue and murder, of hunting and hawking, of art and of literature.

This was the favourite home of the Stuart kings from the time of James II (of Scotland) until 1651, when Charles II left the palace to face defeat and exile. The fate of the palace at that time was equally dismal; it was occupied by Cromwell's troops, damaged by fire and allowed to fall into ruin.

In 1887, though, the 3rd Marquess of Bute, a descendant of the Royal Stuarts, became Hereditary Keeper of the palace. He restored and rebuilt much of the palace and, though it is now in the care of the National Trust for Scotland, his descendant still lives in the building as Keeper. Inside, it is furnished with huge old oak furniture, including a great four-poster bed said to have belonged to James VI, and rich wall hangings. The old library has a remarkable *trompe-l'oeil* ceiling and there are 17th-century Flemish 'Verdure' tapestries along the gallery leading to the King's apartments.

Open from April to October daily. Tel: 01337 857397.

Falkland Palace has a unique royal tennis court which was built for James V in 1539 and pre-dates Henry VIII's court at Hampton Court Palace by more than 80 years.

The great towers are a sturdy feature of this royal palace

Above and right, the largest mansion in Scotland to be inhabited, Floors Castle is set in pleasant gardens above the River Tweed

FLOORS CASTLE
Borders

1 MILE (1.5 KM) NORTH OF KELSO

Floors Castle is enormous – indeed, it is the largest inhabited house in Scotland. It was built in the early 18th century for the 1st Duke of Roxburghe, who played a leading part in the union of Scotland with England in 1707. Doubtless the situation of his home in the Borders coloured his views, for this was a troubled frontier of cross-border skirmishes and moving boundaries for many centuries before the two countries united.

The castle's architect was William Adam, but his creation was enlarged and embellished about a century later by William Playfair, whose many other commissions included the National Gallery in Edinburgh. It was he who added the countless pepper-pot cupolas which give Floors its fairy-tale appearance today. By this time the 6th Duke was in residence, having inherited the title and the estate at the age of just seven years. He was the heir of Sir James Innes,

largely thank his wife, the American heiress Mary Goelet, who devoted herself to the house she had been taken to as a bride in 1903. From her Long Island home she brought the wonderful collection of 17th-century Brussels tapestries which adorn the walls of Floors Castle, and she also acquired the collections of French furniture and contemporary art which enhance the elegant rooms here. The Needle Room, reputedly identical to a room at Versailles, now acts as a gallery for paintings by Matisse, Redon, Bonnard and Augustus John.

The gardens and grounds around Floors Castle are delightful; they contain a holly tree which is said to mark the spot where James II was killed whilst besieging the castle.

Open at Easter, then from late April to October on selected days, but daily in high summer. Tel: 01573 223333.

'... altogether a kingdom for Oberon and Titania to dwell in.'
Sir Walter Scott

Floors Castle was seen world-wide when it appeared as the ancestral home of Tarzan, in the film *Greystoke*

who had won the inheritance after a protracted and very expensive court case during which a number of distant relatives claimed the dukedom. Sir James was 76 years old and childless when he was granted the title and the estate, encouraging many of his unsuccessful rivals to wait eagerly in the wings for a second chance. However, in his 80s he fathered a son, James – the 6th Duke. James both increased the family fortunes and its importance to such an extent that he was honoured with a state visit from Queen Victoria in 1867 – a summer-house in the garden was built especially for her.

Though the exterior of the castle has changed little since the 6th Duke's day, the interior was considerably altered by the 8th Duke around the turn of the century. For the contents we must

GLAMIS CASTLE
Tayside

5 MILES (8 KM) WEST OF FORFAR

'All hail, Macbeth! hail to thee, Thane of Glamis!'. Shakespeare's 'Scottish Play' has made the name of Glamis known to countless generations, but though *Macbeth* was based on real historical events, the setting of Glamis Castle was pure poetic licence. A more suitable location would have been hard to find, though, for the romantically turreted mansion is steeped in the past and its oldest parts have an atmosphere which is entirely conducive to ancient legends and intrigue. And yet the majority of the castle today is a warm and utterly delightful family home, where cosy sofas, masses of fresh flowers and charming family photographs mingle with fine works of art, historic tapestries and reminders of royal connections.

Glamis has been the home of the Earls of Strathmore since 1372, when Sir John Lyon was granted the thaneage by his father-in-law, Robert II, and royalty have frequently been entertained here ever since. In 1923 Lady Elizabeth Bowes Lyon, daughter of the then Earl and Countess of Strathmore, married into the royal family, subsequently to become the Queen of George VI, thus securing royal links with Glamis for many more years to come.

Open from April to October daily. Other times by appointment. Tel: 01307 840242 and 840243.

This fine, multi-turreted castle is famous for its royal connections

HILL OF TARVIT
Fife

2½ MILES (4 KM) SOUTH OF CUPAR

A masterpiece of Edwardian elegance in the best Scottish traditions

When F B Sharp bought the modest house standing on this site at around the turn of the century, then known as Wemyss Hall, he very soon set about creating for himself a much larger house in which to display the considerable collections he had built up. That is not to say that the house was entirely unsuitable. Indeed, in one respect it was the perfect showcase for the beautiful French furniture – it had been designed by Sir William Bruce, a noted Scottish architect who was much influenced by French style.

The house simply wasn't large enough for the extensive belongings of Mr Sharp, which included fine antiques, Flemish tapestries, paintings and Chinese porcelain. He chose Sir Robert Lorimer as his architect and decided to simply fill in the space between the two existing wings.

Each of the new rooms created here was designed specifically to suit their contents, and today they display not only Sharp's splendid antiques, but also illustrate the imaginative skill of the architect and the excellent taste of his employer.

As well as all this, visitors to Hill of Tarvit today can gain an insight into the workings of such a mansion in Edwardian times, notably in the restored laundry. Concerts and art exhibitions are regularly held here.

Open over Easter, then from May to October daily. Tel: 01334 53127.

HOPETOUN HOUSE
Lothian

2 MILES (3 KM) WEST OF SOUTH QUEENSFERRY

A swathe of grassy parkland cuts through the wooded southern shore of the Firth of Forth and at its centre stands one of Scotland's most splendid mansions, Hopetoun House, the home of the Marquess of Linlithgow. Begun in 1699, it is the creation of two of Scotland's most celebrated architects – Sir William Bruce, who was responsible for the original building, and William Adam, who enlarged it some time later.

The Marquess's ancestors, the Hope family, were diligent in their public service and in their studies of the law

The sweeping front of the house, below, and right, richly damasked walls offset Old Masters

and the sciences. In the 17th century Sir Thomas Hope rose to become Charles I's King's Advocate, and his sons followed him into the legal profession. It was his grandson, John Hope, who purchased the land on which Hopetoun House now stands.

Hopetoun's interiors are a sumptuous progression of richly decorated rooms which provide a suitably grand setting for the fine works of art, including notable paintings by such artists as Canaletto, Gainsborough and Raeburn, displayed within them. The red drawing room, with its scarlet damask

wall covering and intricate gilded plaster ceiling, is one of the most magnificent rococo rooms in Scotland, while the gold state dining room is a set piece of the Regency period. Hot food would have been brought here from the kitchen in a steam-heated container, pushed along a railway track, then raised in a lift to a warming oven from where it was served by the butler and footmen. This is also where the family portraits are congregated.

The front stairs are an important feature of the original house and are in complete contrast with the state apartments, having mellow pine panelling with painted panels and borders which are beautifully carved with flowers, fruit, corn stalks and peapods.

One unusual attraction at Hopetoun House is the roof-top viewing platform. The wonderful panorama over the surrounding grounds to the countryside beyond and, of course, the

Forth, with its famous bridges away to the east, is well worth the climb.

Hopetoun also has a number of special exhibitions, including a family museum and 'The Building of Hopetoun', commemorating the architects and craftspeople whose talents combined to create this magnificent building. The contracts and accounts make fascinating reading. Out in the tack room off the courtyard is a display, entitled 'Horse and Man in Lowland Scotland', devoted to the role played by the horse in the economic and social life of the area before the motor vehicle took over.

Open from mid-April to early October daily. Tel: 0131 331 2451.

When King George IV came to Hopetoun in 1822 the ceremonials were masterminded by Sir Walter Scott. With the 4th Earl of Hopetoun as their Captain-General, a company of gentlemen archers formed a guard of honour for the King's arrival. He was so impressed that the company were granted the title of 'King's Bodyguard in Scotland' – a ceremonial role which continues to this day.

INVERARAY CASTLE
Strathclyde

INVERARAY, 19 MILES (31 KM) NORTH-EAST OF LOCHGILPHEAD

The town of Inveraray, always closely linked with the castle, originally clustered around the walls of the ancient keep. When the new castle was built a whole new town was also constructed, but at a greater distance from the clan chief's home. It is a splendid example of 18th-century town planning.

Pepperpot towers distinguish the castle, set just beyond the town of Inveraray

The building of this sumptuous mansion as a replacement for the fortified keep which preceded it marked the beginning of a new era of peace in the area, free of the inter-clan rivalry that had dogged earlier centuries. Inveraray had been the home of the Chief of the Clan Campbell since the 15th century, but the present castle was built in the 18th century for the then Chief, the 3rd Duke of Argyll. Designed by Sir John Vanbrugh, it is a sturdy, square structure with a central square tower and round towers at each corner surmounted by conical roofs. Set amid glorious scenery, it presents an enchanting picture .

There are a series of grand state rooms inside the castle, with elaborate wall paintings and intricate plasterwork, and the state dining room is exceptionally beautiful – very much in the French style which had been popularised at the time by the Prince of Wales. The tapestry room is exquisite, with Beauvais tapestries and delicate ceiling by Robert Adam, while the lofty armoury hall has a magnificent display of arms and armour arranged in great fan and circle patterns. The long, long history of the Campbells is reflected in the genealogical display in the Clan Room.

Open from April to October on most days. Tel: 01499 2203.

LAURISTON CASTLE
Lothian

1 MILE (1.5 KM) EAST OF CRAMOND

Antique furniture, collected at the turn of the century, adorns the house

A particular nightmare of school days for some of us can be directly attributed to Lauriston Castle, for it was John Napier, the son of its first owner, who invented logarithms! The house, set in 30 acres (12ha) of lovely parkland and peaceful gardens, has considerably more charm for most people than the mathematics, however.

A number of notable Scots have called it home over the years, including the 18th-century financier, John Law, who held high office at the Court of pre-revolution France, and William Robert Reid, proprietor of a prestigious firm of cabinet-makers in Edinburgh. The latter was an enthusiastic collector of antiques, fine furniture, prints and other works of art, and he bought Lauriston Castle in 1902 to provide a suitable setting for his collections. In order to preserve their cherished home and its contents intact, Mr and Mrs Reid bequeathed the entire property to the nation in 1926.

The oldest part of the house, a tower-house which now forms the south-west corner of the building, dates back to the late 16th century and includes the lovely Oak Room; the remainder was added in two phases during the 19th century.

Open from April to October daily, except Friday; weekends only in winter. Tel: 0131 336 2060.

A concealed stairway leads from one corner of the Oak Room to a small chamber in the tower wall. It may have been used as a hideaway, but a spy-hole, blocked when a new ceiling was added in 1827, suggests a more sinister purpose.

MELLERSTAIN
Borders

3 MILES (5 KM) SOUTH OF GORDON

This grand and imposing mansion, home of the Earl and Countess of Haddington, was built in two stages – the first by William Adam in 1725 and the second by his more famous son, Robert, in the 1770s.

Although the house is 18th-century through and through, the ancestors of the current Earl and Countess, the Baillies, had owned the estate since 1642. Mixed fortunes in the early years led various members of the family into imprisonment, exile and execution. However, a young and penniless George Baillie fled to Holland to become a junior officer in the Prince of Orange's Horse Guards. When that same Prince of Orange became William III of England,

Pleasing Adam interiors are a major feature of Mellerstain

the family fortunes were restored so they were in a position to create this beautiful home, which has been splendidly preserved in its original style.

The classical interiors are among the finest you will see anywhere – the library has justifiably been hailed as a masterpiece – and the intricate plaster ceilings and panels are exquisite. Elegant furniture and fine paintings more than adequately set off the design and decoration of each of the rooms, and as well as many family portraits the house contains works by Van Dyck, Gainsborough, Ramsay, Aikman and Nasmyth.

Open over Easter, then from May to September daily, except Saturday. Tel: 01573 410225.

SCONE PALACE
Tayside

1 MILE (1.5 KM) NORTH OF PERTH

Scone Palace is inextricably linked with Scotland's historic past

The seat of government in Pictish times, the site of the Stone of Destiny and the place where Scottish kings (including Macbeth and Robert the Bruce) were crowned until 1651 – Scone Palace and the history of Scotland are inextricably linked. Here, great and decisive events took place and powerful men shaped the future. And yet, once the Stone of Destiny had been removed to London, the heart and the power seemed gradually to seep away until, in 1559, the abbey was destroyed by an unruly mob, stirred up by an inflammatory speech by John Knox.

After this, Scone was given to Sir David Murray (later Lord Scone and Viscount Stormont), whose descendants still live there. It was his grandson, the 3rd Earl, who created the Scone Palace we see today, though it was 'Gothicised' in the early 19th century as a tribute to its monastic origins. A series of elegant, beautifully decorated rooms is on show, but even they are overshadowed by the wonderful collections of porcelain, ivories, 16th-century needlework, French furniture and works of art. But though Scone's historical importance and its unrivalled collections might seem overwhelming, it is still very much a family home, with all the charm that entails.

Open from April to October daily. Tel: 01738 552300.

The Stone of Destiny, or Stone of Scone, was taken to Westminster Abbey by Edward I in 1296 and every monarch since that time has been crowned upon it. A local story maintains that Edward was actually fobbed off with an imitation stone, hastily hacked out by the monks at Scone, and that the original lies hidden somewhere in an underground chamber.

TOROSAY CASTLE
Isle of Mull

1 MILE (1.5 KM) SOUTH OF CRAIGNURE

*T*his is no ancient seat of a clan chief, but a creation of the Victorian and Edwardian eras when the Scottish baronial style was enjoying a revival. It was built for one John Campbell, but the cost proved too much and he was forced to sell the house in 1865 to Arbuthnot Charles Guthrie, the great-great-great-uncle of the present owner, Christopher James.

Torosay Castle is a fine home by any standards, but its exceptional charm comes from the mark left here by successive generations of the family and by their obvious love for the place. Visitors here are not confined behind barriers, or trailed around the house at the heels of a guide, but are actually invited to linger and browse through the contents of the family scrapbooks and other items in the archive room, or to have a look through the book of the Devonshire House Ball in the library. Delightful family mementoes are everywhere, from portraits, including a charcoal sketch of Murray Guthrie by John Singer Sargent, to the head of a tiger which was shot by Christopher James's grandmother in India in 1922. Lovely gardens surround the house and include a statue walk, with 19 life-size figures.

Open at Easter, then from late April to mid-October daily. Tel: 01680 2421.

A delightful reflection of Victorian and Edwardian taste

TRAQUAIR HOUSE
Borders

1 MILE (1.5 KM) SOUTH OF INNERLEITHEN

The mellow old house of Traquair began its existence as a royal hunting lodge

Traquair is the oldest inhabited house in Scotland, and it is also among the most romantic. It was built in the 12th century and has been visited by no less than 27 monarchs over the years – William the Lion held court here, and there are particularly strong links with Mary, Queen of Scots and with the Jacobite cause. During the Civil War the then Earl could not quite decide which side to support, and so took no active part himself, but he sent his son to join his kinsman Montrose before the battle of Philiphaugh. Shortly afterwards, however, when the fleeing Montrose sought refuge at Traquair, the Earl pretended he wasn't at home.

The house reflects every moment of its 800 years of history, with ancient stone walls, a 'modern' wing, dating from 1680, and furniture and contents which span many centuries. The Museum Room is particularly absorbing, with items ranging from Mary, Queen of Scots' rosary and crucifix to a 16th-century calculator and a lengthy list (in her own hand) of the 4th Countess's children.

Traquair remains at the heart of a working estate which includes Britain's oldest surviving working brewery, revived to full working order in 1965.

Open Easter week, then from May to September daily. Tel: 01896 830785.

The large Bear Gates, once the main entrance to Traquair, were closed in 1745, not to be re-opened until there was once again a Stuart on the throne. Ever since that day a new drive to the house, running parallel to the old avenue, has been used.

The wind through the rusted
iron sings,
The sun on the self-sown
tangle burns,
But never a hoof on the
roadway rings -
The gate is shut till the King
returns.'
W H Ogilvie

INDEX